UNITY LIBRARY & ARCHIVES
Liberal Christian orthodoxy.

C0-AMA-500

6/
63

LIBERAL CHRISTIAN ORTHODOXY

Liberal
Christian Orthodoxy

by

F. H. CLEOBURY, Ph.D.(London)

JAMES CLARKE & CO. LTD.
33 STORE STREET, LONDON, W.C.I

UNITY SCHOOL LIBRARY
Unity Village
Lee's Summit, Missouri 64063

First published 1963

© F. H. CLEOBURY, 1963

Made in Great Britain. Printed at the St Ann's Press
Park Road, Altrincham

BR
123
C 594l

Preface

I AM a member of the Council of the Modern Churchmen's Union, and I have been encouraged to write this book by some of my fellow-members. But it is in no sense an official exposition of the Union's views; I alone am responsible for it.

My main motives in writing the book will, I hope, become clear to its readers. But one further motive I may mention here. I am an ordained minister of the Church of England, and in view of the course of recent theological thought in this country, as outlined in the first chapter, I am anxious to make it clear to the general public that the interpretation of Anglican doctrine set forth in this book is within the permitted limits. This is by no means clear to the average layman today; indeed, the Report on *Doctrine in the Church of England*, issued in 1938 as the result of the labours of the Doctrinal Commission set up in 1922, has been pigeon-holed and largely forgotten. I believe that a large number of intelligent people in this country are sincerely drawn towards the Church, but hesitate to identify themselves with it so long as they would thereby be deemed to hold beliefs which even the most cautious thinkers must feel to be impossible for the modern mind.

F. H. CLEOBURY

The Rectory
Hertingfordbury
January 1962

Contents

Introduction

To SOME, the title of this book will appear contradictory. For the word "orthodoxy" suggests adherence to tradition and the word "liberalism", in the field of religion, suggests departure from it. But "orthodoxy" does not *mean* adherence to tradition; it means correctness of doctrine, and to maintain such correctness may involve, in theology as in science, a willingness to learn. There is, then, no formal contradiction in the claim to be both liberal and orthodox.

But liberals have not usually stressed the importance of orthodoxy. The reason for my stressing it is that there is a notion abroad that all religions mean the same "underneath" and that the religion of the future must be the highest common factor of all religions—a vague, creedless uplift. This is not my view. Every student of logic knows that there are pairs of propositions which are strict contradictories; one of them must be true and the other false. I believe that there is strict contradiction between essential Christianity and the religions of the East in certain vital matters, and that Christianity is right. It is precisely because liberalism involves a willingness to criticize one's own religion that the liberal has the right to demand that those who profess religions other than his shall criticize theirs, and has the right to do it for them if they will not do it for themselves.

A glance at the chapter headings may suggest a lack of unity in the book. There is, however, a real unity of purpose underlying it, although it does not profess to exhibit a deductive progress in which each chapter is an inference from what precedes. The argument is not a chain in which the conclusion is contained in the last link; it is, rather, a wheel in which the truth lies at the centre, and each chapter works inwards along a different spoke. The central creed is a simple one; true religion, as I see it, depends on believing two or three things intensely—not on accepting a complex of dogma.

I am primarily a philosopher, not a dogmatic theologian. I share the conviction of contemporary philosophers in the English-speaking world that philosophical and theological writings in the past have contained far too many assertions to the verification or falsification of which no human experience is really relevant. Obscurity and dullness have too often been taken for profundity. In the course of fifty years of adult thought I have had to ponder over many abstruse questions, but I am now realizing that what I have really cared about, and wanted to be sure of, is the creed I learned from my mother— that there is a good God, revealed to us in Jesus, and that therefore death can be for us the gateway to a better life than this. This creed is both simple and vital. Those whose lives are lived in an intense conviction of its truth are a class apart from those who deny it or ignore it.

Unity of aim in a book, or in a life study, can be secured by confining oneself to one examinable subject, such as physics or metaphysics or history. But the unity can be of a different kind; there will be unity if studies in a number of different fields are all being directed towards an answer to one concrete question. To revert to our analogy of the wheel, I regard this question as the hub; the various spokes of approach may be metaphysics, philosophical analysis, physics, history—particularly the study of Christian origins—and psychical research.

So much, then, for the unity of the book. The various chapters are working from diverse directions to a common centre. And although the discussions may at first glance appear complicated, the aim is simple and clear. The complications are not of my creation; many of them are the sophistries of Greek and Oriental speculation. But to unravel them properly requires patience.

The aim at simplicity will also be apparent, I hope, in my treatment of the doctrine of the Incarnation. I hold it to be the answer to the deepest human needs, and yet we have to teach it to simple people. The Church, on the whole, is failing to distinguish between the essential doctrines of the Faith, which are soundly based, and claims in the field of history which, because dubious, are embarrassments. It is these claims which give so many people the impression that in contrast with science, which is out for truth, religion is out for comfort, or for supplying an emotional driving-force for ethics. We desperately need comfort and moral motive, but they must be grounded in truth.

CHAPTER 1

Christian Liberalism Today

IT IS sometimes said that the Christian liberalism of the late Victorian and the Edwardian ages is outmoded. And it is customary to date the outmoding from the appearance of a work by Albert Schweitzer, completed in 1906 and published in English in 1910 under the title *The Quest of the Historical Jesus*.

Is this true? It depends on how you use the word "liberalism". It is sometimes used to connote the view that Jesus was a teacher of ethical theism—our duty to love God, and our neighbour as ourselves—and that the overlaying of this simple teaching by teaching which identified Jesus with the Son of Man, soon to come in the clouds of heaven and bring in the End of the Age, was entirely due to the early Church. Now if we define "liberalism", thus, it is true that Johannes Weiss and Schweitzer raised grave objections to it. But this did not mean that Schweitzer's work vindicated religious *conservatism*. Schweitzer moved farther from orthodoxy than had the liberals. Schweitzer did not contest the main liberal thesis that ethical theism is essential Christianity, and that for the modern man Christianity must be stripped of the first century brand of eschatology. But he affirmed that the outlook of Jesus *himself* was conditioned by this eschatology which we can no longer accept, and that Jesus himself announced as imminent the manifestation of the supernatural Kingdom of God, and the coming of the Son of Man in the clouds. The liberals had said that ethical theism was essential Christianity and that that is what Jesus taught. Schweitzer did not contest the view that for us today ethical theism is essential Christianity. He merely denied that that was all that Jesus taught, and said that Jesus shared the limitations of his age.

That this summary of Schweitzer's position is not inaccurate may be seen from Chapter VI of his book *My Life and Thought*, particularly page 72 and the following passage on page 74: "The religion of love taught by Jesus has been freed from any dogmatism which clung to it, by the disappearance of the late-Jewish eschatological world-view." Schweitzer quite clearly held that to get at essential Christianity we must free it from first-century thought-forms; but whereas most scholars had held that these thought-forms had been due to the early Church, Schweitzer attributed them to Jesus himself. If, then, you define "liberalism" as the belief that Jesus taught pure ethical theism unmixed with eschatology, then you can say that Schweitzer's work has outmoded liberalism. But you cannot claim that it strengthened conservatism. Quite the reverse!

But the definition of Christian liberalism which we have so far considered is by no means the only one. Liberalism should be defined more broadly, and then we can see that it has by no means been undermined. I would define it as the view that although historical criticism has made it impossible to claim that certain details traditionally believed to be essential to the *kerygma*, the gospel proclamation, were authentic history, this is gain rather than loss, for some of these details are, in our day, not only not essential to the *kerygma* but embarrassments to it. We hold that the human tragedy of the twentieth century witnesses more strongly to the relevance and truth of the Christian diagnosis of the human situation than does any appeal to physical miracles in the first century.

Another way of answering the question, "What is liberalism?" is to consider the question, "Why do we believe the Christian religion to be the highest revelation from God to man?" If a person replies, "I believe it because it is taught by an infallible authority," whether he means the Pope, the Church or the Bible, he is not a liberal. This is not to say that the liberal, as such, denies that *in any sense* the Church or the Bible speaks with authority. It is merely that what the liberal thinks about the Church or the Bible is just one of his Christian beliefs—coherent with them but not the sole reason for believing them. I have heard of a Catholic remarking to a Protestant, "We believe broadly the same theology, but you believe it for the insufficient reason that you judge it true, while I believe it for the sufficient reason that the Church teaches it." And some of my conservative evangelical friends seem to think that the necessary and sufficient reason for believing anything in the field of religion is that it can be "proved from scripture".

Now it is not logically impossible that a whole corpus of beliefs should base themselves on a fundamental belief in an infallible authority—Pope or Church or Bible. But the question arises, how does one arrive at the fundamental belief? If one is going to bow to this basic authority one must surely hold that one is, and has a right to be, more immediately certain of the infallibility of this authority than one could be of any of the doctrines which, so to speak, are mediated to one via this authority. He who holds as fundamental the acceptance of the infallibility of the Church or the Bible, and who argues that without such a basic belief the other items of the Christian creed are mere matters of human argument or "private judgment", must logically hold that acceptance of the infallibility of Church or of Bible is *not* a mere matter of human argument or private judgment. He must maintain that this basic belief is a matter of immediate conviction, possibly unanalyzable but certain and inescapable, for those to whom God's Spirit may reveal it. It seems to me, indeed, that he is bound logically to go even farther, and hold that anyone in good faith who prays for guidance can reach an intuitive certainty that the Pope, the Church or the Bible (as the case may be) has infallible authority.

Now, as I say, there is nothing impossible about this. But it does not seem to me to accord with the facts, or with the workings of the human mind or of the Spirit of God. I am far from denying—indeed, I affirm earnestly—that faith comes to us from experiences which convince us in some "immediate" way that certain statements are true. There are flashes of insight, of conviction, which are not *merely* rational but are also highly emotional. A rational element there *must* be, for we cannot believe the contradictory, the incoherent and the unevidenced, but our emotions—our deep needs and satisfactions—are themselves part of the evidence. I think that in these experiences we jump to a synthesis by a sort of mental instinct, the rationality of which we can analyze afterwards. Let us, for convenience, call these experiences "intuitions". Then we can say that after we have come to our faith by such intuitions, we can reasonably believe that they were not merely human constructions, but that they were revelations—that at these moments we were indwelt by the Spirit of God.

But is it true that it is only the infallibility of Pope, Church or Bible that is conveyed to us at such moments? Is it true that our beliefs about Jesus and his cross cannot be established by such experiences, cannot, that is, be established *immediately*, but must be mediated by a previous immediate conviction about the infallibility of an "authority"? To ask this question is to see the answer. It is completely untrue.

It would be far easier to defend the thesis that it is faith in Christ that is basic, and that theories of infallibility and authority involve human argument at a lower level altogether.

In short, I cannot evade the responsibility of making decisions by relying on an authority. For there are a number of authorities inviting my allegiance—Pope, Christian Councils, Bible, Koran, Upanishads. To choose between them is my responsibility. If the pejorative label "private judgment" is applicable anywhere, it is applicable here. If you say. "No, for your decision can be prompted by the Spirit of God," I must ask, "Why cannot my acceptance of *any* article of the Christian creed be prompted by the Spirit of God?"

So much in explanation, and very broadly in defence, of Christian liberalism. Let us now notice some of the reactions to the work of Schweitzer. He said, in effect, that an attempt to "go behind" the early Church to the historical Jesus was an embarrassment to traditionalism, not a help. The reaction of some of those determined at all costs to maintain the tradition was to proclaim that it was *impossible* to go behind the tradition! Broadly speaking, there were two schools who took this line, both of them influenced by Kierkegaard's existentialism. Far from combating the thesis that the written gospels contain the early church's *interpretation* of Jesus and are not bare, factual history, they gloried in it.

The first school presented the synoptic and the fourth gospels as telling a more or less harmonious story; we cannot discriminate between what is and what is not historical; we can take it as a whole or leave it. When it is preached, men are confronted or challenged by God; this is a fact of experience, and it vindicates the essential historicity of the tradition. The foregoing is probably a fair summary of the Barth-Brunner position as interpreted by the main stream of Anglicanism. The other school, represented by Bultmann, also says that we cannot, in a sense, "go behind" traditional *theology*. But this, for them, does not mean that we cannot criticize traditional *history* and first-century thought-forms. Indeed, Christianity needs de-mythologizing. But it does mean that when all the criticism and de-mythologizing is done, we are still confronted by a system of dogma, largely Pauline, which we cannot "go behind"— which we must accept as having Divine authority.

Both these forms of neo-orthodoxy are open to criticism. With regard to the first, we may agree that the preaching of the Christian faith is a challenge to the conscience of men, and that in hearing the gospel, men can feel that they are confronted by God, or by Divine truth. But this does not absolve us from the task of trying to distinguish the kernel from the husk, the historically certain from the uncertain, the Divine treasure from the human earthen vessel; the Bible bears many marks of its human origin. And we strongly deny that it is impossible to "go behind" the Gospel accounts. In answer to the second

B

school we may say, "You admit, in effect, the necessity for discriminating between the human and the Divine elements in the New Testament. But why, when we have de-mythologized the kerygma, must we either accept or reject as a whole an alleged closely integrated *corpus* of doctrine labelled "New Testament theology", largely based on St. Paul? This is not to say that the liberal, as such, repudiates St. Paul. Many of us feel that his essential insights were valuable and true. But his teachings, even when de-mythologized, do not form such a close unity that they must be accepted or rejected *as a whole*.

The man in the pew, and the reader of church periodicals, are frequently assured nowadays that the "destructive" criticism of fifty years ago is outmoded. For example, an outline of the liberal interpretation of Christian origins which I recently published[1] was described by one critic as "a plea for the antiquated modernism of fifty years ago". Without coming down to any details, he remarked that I had been greatly influenced by B. W. Bacon. The latter he dismissed by a reference to Processor Denney's description of him as "a wild man"—a verdict with which "most scholars now agree". Actually, of course, Bacon was a profound scholar and thinker. His work *The Fourth Gospel in Research and Debate*, if it is to be refuted at all, demands an almost page-by-page refutation, which it has never received. He cannot be dismissed with an epithet. And we can set over against the conservative reaction the writings of S. G. F. Brandon, John Knox, F. C. Grant, and a number of others. Indeed, if we consider his work in the field of Christian origins and ignore his existentialist theology, we can claim Bultmann as a support of the liberal approach.

One curious feature of the study of Christian origins in recent years is that few non-Christian scholars appear to be working at it; it has largely got into the hands of the clergy. Studies by writers frankly hostile to Christianity are few and far between. Fifty years ago F. C. Conybeare, an Oxford scholar of European reputation and a Fellow of the British Academy, published a

---

[1] *The Armour of Saul.* James Clarke, 1957.

"rationalist" *History of New Testament Criticism*, and followed this with *Myth, Magic and Morals*, but I know of no Oxford or Cambridge scholar who, during the last two decades, has produced an outstanding *anti*-Christian work on Christian origins. The explanation, I suggest, is simple; it is that the emotional urge to attack Christianity has largely vanished. Non-Christian scholars have largely lost the confidence which they certainly had in the Victorian and Edwardian periods that the Christian ethic could survive the destruction of the Christian faith. Scholars who approve of Christian ethics are therefore unwilling to spend energy in criticizing those elements in the tradition which *the masses* have been taught to regard as the pillars of Christianity.

An example of this attitude can, I think, be seen in the case of the late Gilbert Murray. There can be no doubt about his views on Christian origins. When L. P. Jacks published, in 1948, a translation of Alfred Loisy's *La Naissance du Christianisme* under the title *The Birth of the Christian Religion*, Murray contributed a preface in which he describes this work as "the most masterly of all the attempts to understand and describe according to the canons of human history, without prejudice and without miracle, a movement which has shaped the whole subsequent religion of the Western World." If this great scholar and humanist had chosen to devote to a sustained attack on the traditional view of Christian origins the energy which he spent in the cause of international peace, we should not be hearing today the facile generalizations in fundamentalist quarters about "antiquated modernism". I am very far from suggesting that Loisy's and Murray's theories of Christian origins have to be accepted. Indeed, my own studies have convinced me that writers like Schweitzer and Loisy exaggerated the place of apocalyptic in our Lord's thought; his ethical teaching was by no means merely an "interims-ethik". Nor do I think it impossible, by a careful study of the gospels, to arrive at a soundly based knowledge of the events of the last months of our Lord's life, and of his conception of his mission. I do not think we can concede as history all that the traditionalist demands, but neither need we leave the radical critic in possession of the field. All that I am urging at this point is that we must take criticism seriously; we cannot just brush it aside. I am firmly convinced that all that a firmly based Christian philosophy *needs* to claim as historically certain *can* be claimed as historically certain. But it is foolish and wrong to claim as certain what any honest scholar knows to be debatable. For example, are we wise to let our children form the impression that faith in God's revelation in Christ is bound up with acceptance of the birth stories in Matthew and Luke? Some of us find it difficult to write on this point dispassionately. We remember the bitter heart-searchings of our later adolescence.

The liberal Christian has to meet criticism not only from within the Church but also from non-Christians. The following is typical:

> "As for modernism, how can one have any devotion to what is a mere smell, and that a not very attractive one? or respect for the processes of peeling the onion—while holding on to all the emoluments and privileges."[2]

Another example of this modern tendency is the recent habit of non-Christian writers to sneer at Kingsley and patronize Newman in the matter of their famous controversy. Dare one guess that what annoys anti-Christians with Christian liberalism is their subconscious awareness that it may well prove, in the long run, the one strong force with which they have to reckon

---

[2] A. L. Rowse, *A Cornish Childhood*. A charge brought against us in these terms hardly merits a reply. But it occurs in a moving and sincere chapter in a fascinating book. One can only wonder that when he wrote it in 1942 the author had failed to realize that others may, like him, have been thrilled in childhood by the beauty of the drama of the Christian liturgy, and yet, unlike him, have been passionately convinced that underlying this beauty there was truth. They did not think they were peeling an onion till nothing remained; they thought and still think, they were removing the shell and that the kernel remains. I doubt if any of our clergy have come into the church for "emoluments and privileges", but if there are such they are not likely to join the Modern Churchmen's Union!

—that while they can afford to await the self-destruction of a faith which bases itself on dubious history, they may find impregnable a faith which applies the canons of historical enquiry quite impartially and preaches Christianity as the deepest and truest philosophy of life?

But let us return to the theologians. The irony of much theological thinking in the English-speaking world in the last two or three decades is that not merely has it loaded upon history a burden which history cannot bear, but it has joined with sceptics in denigrating Christian philosophy. We are confronted by a spectacle which we should deem amazing were we suddenly confronted by it and had we not gradually drifted into it—namely that stupendous statements about the nature and work of God are being made by men who deny that there are *reasons* for believing that God exists! Many of these theologians would resent having their views classed with those of Professor R. B. Braithwaite.[3] But there is this in common between Braithwaite and Christians who disparage any appeal to metaphysics to justify belief in God. They have all shifted the emphasis from ontology, the doctrine of *being*, to a justification of God-*language* as an interpretation of human experience.

Professor Braithwaite holds that statements about God are merely elliptical statements about human attitudes, intentions and feelings. Talk about God should not imply any belief in a cosmological God who exists "outside" us—an objective Entity Who corresponds to the word "God" just as a real and objective Mr. Jones corresponds to the words "Mr. Jones". Few of these theologians display Braithwaite's bluntness in the matter, but he is only carrying to its logical conclusion the thesis which regards God-language as an interpretation of human experience whilst denying that such interpretation has any strictly *rational* grounds. We are told in certain quarters that the statement "God is Love" must be taken literally—that the word "God" is only a synonym for "love"; we must not think of God as an objective Mind Who is loving. The existentialist, in his turn,

[3] *An Empiricist's View of the Nature of Religious Belief.* C.U.P., 1957.

tells us that we must distrust any reasoning to the effect that the ultimate Source and Ground of existence is personal or super-personal; we somehow, he tells us, become "immediately" *aware* of God in an "encounter"—through some experience which challenges us to an act of faith.

I find acute difficulty with these attitudes, and I think most plain men, and indeed most intelligent and scholarly people who are not theologians or philosophers, feel it too. They will not continue to say, "I believe in God" unless they mean an *objective* Mind. I can state my intention to lead an "agapeistic" life (*pace* Professor Braithwaite) without using God-language, and if I ceased to believe in such an objective Mind I should deem it silly to throw my language into the God-form. And I can make no sense of the notion of an objective love which is not the love displayed by an objective Person; "love" is an abstract noun. And so far as the existentialist's "encounter" is concerned, the simple truth is that we cannot have an *immediate* awareness of a human or a divine being. I can have a feeling of, I can be immediately aware of, a colour or a smell, but a mental process which issues in the statement "John exists" or "God exists", is vastly more complex. There is here an intellectual construction. It is a sheer abuse of language to say that a person can have a *feeling* of the presence of God, if the word "feeling" is meant to exclude thinking. In interpreting any human experience *of God*, we are making an intellectual judgment. If there are no *reasons* for believing in an objective God, this intellectual judgment has no secure intellectual basis; we have no sound ground on which to pass from a psychological to a theological treatment of our experience.

We have, then, to get back to philosophical theism—a study in which our appeal to human psychology and human history *is not an alternative to*, but *a part of*, a rational metaphysical construction. This will mean that when we make the concessions to historical criticism which honesty demands, we shall in no sense be retreating; we shall be moving to a stronger position from which an offensive can be begun. It will mean that although we cannot honestly claim as authentic history all the statements about his person and work attributed to Jesus in the fourth gospel, and although we cannot claim, on the basis of statements peculiar to the first gospel, which reached its present form long after the crucifixion, that Jesus intended to found a church in the traditionalist sense of that word, nevertheless there are the strongest grounds for believing in God and for viewing the course of theistic thought recorded in the Old and New Testaments as containing His revelation.

CHAPTER 2

Is There a Rational Case for Theism?

IT IS by no means unusual nowadays to hear people decrying the use of reason in religion, and urging the claims of our emotional natures. People who talk like this have at the back of their minds something valid and important, but they are expressing it in quite the wrong way. For their language suggests that we should put our rational faculties to sleep and try to believe whatever our emotional natures regard as desirable. Such a suggestion rightly arouses the contempt of the honest man. But these people are perfectly right if what they mean is that our emotional life and our instinctive demands on life furnish data which our rational faculties can use in constructing a sound philosophy—data as valid and far more relevant than the data supplied by the physical sciences. We should never *contrast* emotion with reason, still less pretend that emotion can be a substitute for reason, but we have every right to insist that our rational faculties, just because they *are* rational, must take account of *all* the facts in constructing a philosophy of life, including the facts of human psychology.

I have spoken of our *constructing* a philosophy of life. It is important to insist that all our beliefs about the real world— not only religious beliefs but the beliefs of scientists—are mental constructions. In all cases we survey certain data—certain facts, and we then build up a set of concepts which will, as we say, account for or explain or interpret the facts. This applies to the beliefs of our everyday life—the belief of the jury that a certain person is guilty, a man's belief that his wife loves him, a scientist's belief that this or that theory is true, and even one's belief that other people exist besides oneself.

Why am I labouring this point? Surely, you will say, it is obvious. The answer is that, unfortunately, the whole subject has been bedevilled by the philosopher Descartes—which is all the sadder because he was a great man and said some very important and true things. Descartes held that the only really valid human knowledge was the sort of knowledge you get in pure mathematics—Euclid, for example. What so fascinated him about this sort of reasoning was that he thought it started with self-evident truths, which cannot be doubted, let alone denied, without throwing oneself into self-contradiction, and that it proceeded by inferential steps each one of which, equally, could not be impugned without self-contradiction. He thought that that was the ideal knowledge, and that nothing short of that was worth calling knowledge.

Now Descartes' ideal has been proved illusory. Modern philosophers have shown that the kind of reasoning which Descartes thought was the ideal kind tells us nothing about the real world of things and people, the concrete world around us. It is abstract, and it is hypothetical. Even Euclid does not, in itself, tell us truths about the spatial relations of *physical* objects. It only tells us what would be true *if* physical objects *were* Euclidian. The question whether physical objects *are* Euclidian has to be decided by experiment; and, as you know, there are experimental data which suggest that they are not. The only way of discovering truths about the real world is by observation or experiment, and then thinking out some form of mental construction which will, as we say, "account for" or "interpret" the facts. This is the method used in physics and chemistry and astronomy, in the law-courts, and in our everyday commerce with each other. And by this method we never achieve the 100 per cent theoretical certainty with which we know that Euclid's abstract conclusions follow from his abstract premises. Certainty about the real world is always a matter of *degree*. At the lowest end of the scale there is the scientist's mere working hypothesis, which he frankly states to be merely tentative, a mere guide to his experiments, and which he is perfectly ready to discard if the experiment contradicts it. Half-way up the scale is the type of belief which we think highly probable; we should be greatly surprised if some fact turned up which contradicted it. And at the top of the scale there are beliefs about which we are, and have every right to be, what I would call psychologically certain as distinct from *logically* certain. What is the difference between logical certainty and psychological certainty? We can be logically certain that the conclusion of a proposition of Euclid follows from the premises, for if we affirm the premises and deny the conclusion we can be shown to contradict ourselves. And we can be logically certain because the whole business is abstract, and does not profess to be describing the real concrete world. But when we are thinking about the real world, as in the sciences and history and metaphysics—or in everyday life for that matter—we normally have to be satisfied with mental constructions our denial of which would not land us in self-contradiction; there is always the theoretical possibility that some other theory would equally well account for the facts. Our certainty is psychological, not logical. For example, if you let yourself into your house and are greeted by a lady whom you take to be your wife, you do not say to yourself, "How do I *know* this is my wife? She may be my wife's double, and a practical joke may be being played on me." Of course you do not. You take a chance on it. But the fact remains that your belief that this is your wife is a mental construct to account for the visual sensations you are experiencing; you do not really *see* your wife; you only see patches of colour. You cannot produce the kind of proof which has Euclidian or deductive certainty that it is your wife. But you nevertheless can be certain with a different kind of certainty. The same goes for my belief that other people exist beside myself. It is not *logically* certain that other people exist; it is psychologically certain.

Now my reason for labouring this point is that I have often been shocked by hearing Christians concede quite cheerfully that one cannot prove that God exists. One even hears this sort of remark in the pulpit. I tremble to think of the harm that must be done thereby in an age in which it is firmly believed that science has proved all sorts of interesting and important things about the Universe. The impression given is that science gives us facts while religion merely doles out comfort—that religion is wishful thinking and a desperate attempt to discover some sort of emotional driving force for morals.

Cannot prove that God exists? What kind of proof have you in mind? Rigid deduction from self-evident premises? Well, if we are going to use the word "prove" in *that* way we cannot prove that God exists, but equally the scientist cannot prove any of his statements about natural laws either, and equally I cannot prove to myself that other people exist besides myself. But if you are using the word "prove" in the sense in which it is used every day in the science laboratory, the law-courts, the market-place and our homes—if, that is, you mean "proving" a statement in the sense of showing that it fits or accounts for what we experience, and that there is no alternative theory which fits so well, then it is sheer bias, or muddle-headedness, to deny in principle that God's existence can be proved. One has the right, of course, to criticize any *particular* proof of God's existence if one thinks it invalid. But it is merely silly to rule out all proofs of God in advance on the ground that they cannot be logically necessary deductions.

I will now briefly indicate the way in which I believe it possible to construct a sound rational case for theism. In describing it as sound, I am not, of course, suggesting that the mere statement of it will convince everybody. No one can be convinced of anything unless he is willing to face all the evidence—to weigh it without bias. And in this matter of belief in God the natural man is strongly tempted *not* to face all the evidence. It is quite a mistake to think that wishful thinking operates only in the direction of inducing *belief* in God and the life of the world to come. There is quite as much wishful thinking behind scepticism. Religious belief entails self-discipline and even self-sacrifice. Men very often do not want to pay the price, and they rationalize their unwillingness as honest doubt.

I have found by experience that children of the age of eight years are capable of asking us "Who made God?" or "Did He make Himself?" or "How did He get there to start with?" At the very start, then, of any attempt to state the rational case for Theism, one ought to indicate one's answer to this sort of question.

To begin with, the question itself is wrong. There can, as every student of logic knows, be wrong questions as well as wrong answers. There can, that is, be questions which commit the fallacy of "Many Questions"; they assume or imply what is false, and they must be broken down and re-stated before they can be answered. The stock instance is the question, "Have you given up beating your wife?" Now this question about God commits this fallacy. It assumes that by the word "God" we mean just one entity in a world of entities—a being whose life, like ours, is a series of events within the time series, This assumption is false. We could go even farther and say that the question is self-contradictory, like asking to be shown the corner of the round table.

Let us notice, furthermore, that it is not only people who talk of the ultimate reality as "God" who find it hard to put their metaphysic over to small children. Atheists and theists are in the same boat here. If you claim that the ultimate source of all that exists is "energy" or "matter" or a field of sensa and sensibilia—"neutral stuff"—you will still have to answer your small child's question "How did it get there in the first place?"

The simple truth is that our finite intellects are not capable of explaining why *anything* should be. Our preference for Theism over Atheism is not that it is a better *explanation* of *why* the universe is, but that it is a better *description* of *what* the universe is. We claim that if we are to be true to *all* the facts we shall need the concept of a cosmic mind.

Let us start from the fact that there seem, broadly speaking, to be two different kinds of events. There seem to be material or physical events—such as particles in motion, energy, waves—and there are mental or conscious events such as seeing and hearing, reasoning, feeling angry or happy or sad. Now although there seem to be these quite different sorts of events, there is, nevertheless, an obvious connection between them. They all form part of one Universe. For example, our seeing is a seeing of material objects; our knowing is true of—corresponds to—the material world. The seeing and knowing of material things can occasion mental joy or sorrow, and a mental decision can produce changes in the material world. This means that there are not two really separate realms: a material realm and a mental realm. There is really only one realm, and our task is to try to see it as a unity. For example, if on renting a house you find that in the kitchen there is an indicator which can tell you from which of the rooms a bell is being rung, you assume connection between push-buttons and the indicator; they are not separate machines; they form a unity; there is really only *one* machine. Similarly mental existence and physical existence seem to form a unified system, or a systematic unity.

Now corresponding to the two apparent realms, the physical on the one hand and the mental or psychological on the other, there are, or at any rate there could be, two languages. We could have a language from which all mental or psychological words, such as "choose", "see", "smell", "rejoice", "feel sad", were excluded. It would contain only words for material objects such as chairs, bodily organisms or their parts, nerves, cells, glands—and words like "force", "molecule", "temperature", "entropy", and other technical terms used in mechanics, physics or chemistry. It could speak of "living organisms", but the word "living" here would not connote any mental or psychological quality such as feeling or seeing or choosing; it would describe only how particles forming the organism were connected and how they moved. The whole language would, in effect, describe the world as made up of particles or waves in motion. On the other hand, there could be a language which

contained only those psychological words which the first
language excludes—language about seeing, hearing, deciding,
rejoicing, and so on.

Now the acute reader will almost certainly object to our
second language on the ground that it could not be a *language*
at all. You cannot have a sentence beginning "I see . . ." or "I
perceive . . ." without having, as grammatical object, a mater-
ial-object like "chair". My answer is this. It is true that I need
the whole sentence "I perceive *a chair*", but this *can* describe a
purely mental state. It can mean "I perceive a chair-percept".
And this is what, for the purpose of my second language, I
define it as meaning. "I perceive a chair", *in this language*, describes my state of mind in which "in" my mind, metaphorically
speaking, there is a sensory chair-picture, a chair-percept, a
mental object.

The word "chair", then, can function as either of two quite
distinct symbols, according as it is used in the first or the
second language. It can stand for what is conceived to be a
chair-in-itself, i.e. a chair "outside" or independent of anyone's
perception of it; this is how it functions in the first of our two
languages. Or it can stand for something else, for we can, of
course, make words mean what we like, so long as, unlike
Humpty-Dumpty, who wanted to make "glory" mean a knock-
down argument, we have a reasonable end in view. And so we
can deliberately choose to use a form of language in which the
word "chair" stands for a mental object, a chair-percept "in"
someone's mind. (It is vital to notice that when we talk about
things being "outside" or "inside" the mind we are using metaphors. We must not think of the mind as a kind of pot with
things literally inside it.) This second language can be quite
reasonably justified. We all agree that each one of us perceives
a perceptual continuum. Let us therefore conceive of a language which confines itself to this fact and does not have any
words for material objects-in-themselves—for objects conceived, that is, as existing apart from any experience whatever.

Let us summarize our argument so far. We noted the fact

that the material realm and the mental realm are so closely inter-connected that they must *in some sense* be one realm. We then saw our task to be to see *how* the two are connected. We then noticed that we could have a language which *excluded* all psychological words, and another which consisted of *only* psychological words. It is very natural, then, to inquire whether our task of finding the connection between the two realms can be solved by seeing whether it is possible to "reduce" either of these languages to the other, i.e. to show that what is said in one of the languages can be translated into, or said equally well in, the other, in such wise that we shall be saying the same thing in different words.

Now it is quite clear that the second, the psychological, language cannot thus be reduced to the first. To say that a person feels a pain or is enjoying a pleasant smell is not "saying the same thing" as to say that particles in his brain are moving in a certain way. The first language does not cover all facts; it leaves out the psychological ones. But can the first language be reduced to the second? Some of the profoundest philosophers in the modern world have answered "Yes". And I am going to show that they are right. It can be done. If a man claims that sentences in the impersonal language can be quite adequately translated into sentences in the personal or psychological language, there is no way of proving him wrong; there are no facts which falsify his thesis. This is a point of absolute finality. This is because the issue is philosophical, not scientific. In science we are most reluctant to claim finality for any hypothesis, for even if we are so sure about it that we begin to call it a "law" we must admit, in principle, that it could be falsified by events. But a philosophical problem, by its very nature, can be settled once for all. The best way to show this is to give examples, and we have, in fact, an example before us.

Now to say that the first language can be reduced to the second is to say that any sentence of the first language can be claimed to be an elliptical way of uttering a statement in the second language. Sentences like, "This is chair is heavy" or

"There are mountains on that side of the moon which is invisible from the earth", can be interpreted as convenient ways of uttering less manageable sentences in the second language—sentences about perceptual experiences which conscious beings are having, have had, will have or could reasonably expect to have in certain circumstances. "This chair is heavy" can be interpreted as "If anyone operates on his perceptual continuum in the way which everyday language describes as 'lifting the chair' he will have the feeling which everyday language calls 'muscular strain'." I am not denying that the second way of talking would here be very clumsy and inconvenient. Indeed, the first language doubtless "evolved" in the way it did because it was so convenient. Language came into existence as a tool, something to assist us in the task which everyone has of co-ordinating his actions on his perceptual continuum with that of others on theirs. (For example, primitive men had to help one another to move heavy objects.) But as soon as the human race had reached a stage when men had the leisure and the desire for speculation, for discovering truth for its own sake, the perennial philosophical problems emerged, and it is only of recent years that we have come to see that a system of word-symbols which was created for *practical* ends can quite reasonably be expected to need criticism before the speculative problems can be dealt with effectively.

Any sentence, then, about the properties or relations of material objects can be claimed to be elliptical language about conscious experiences—about what we have experienced, are experiencing, shall experience or can reasonably expect to experience. Such a claim can never be falsified, for it is a matter of philosophy, not science. No possible perceptual experience could be relevant to the disproof of the claim. We have here reached a point of absolute finality. It will always be perfectly possible and reasonable to interpret the Universe in purely personal terms.

The point I am making is easy to misunderstand and has, in fact, often been misunderstood. It is sometimes said that this way of looking at the Universe dissolves away the solid real world and leaves us with a mere flux of ideas and opinions, with no way of distinguishing between what we perceive and what we imagine. But this is a complete misrepresentation. I am not asserting that all I am aware of is a flux of sensations; I am aware of a very solid resisting world—a continuous world. But it is world-for-me; world-for-me is not the same as world-for-you. For example, I may perceive a circle and you, when looking at what we agree to call "the same object" may perceive an oval. But a circle is not an oval. We are not perceiving the same world. We can, in order to account for the relation between what you perceive and what I perceive, postulate a common world-in-itself. But this is not what we *perceive*: it is merely a theoretical object—an object of abstract thought. Each of us perceives only his own perceived-world; we merely *conceive* of a common world-in-itself. But since impersonal language can be regarded as elliptical personal language, it follows that we are in no wise bound to conceive of a material world-in-itself in the sense of dead "matter".

But this is not to deny objectivity and relapse into a subjectivity in which truth and reality vanish. There are, unquestionably, objective laws regulating the order in which my percepts come to me; my powers of selection are very strictly limited. And these laws also govern the connection between my perceptual field and yours; I can often infer, from my percepts and from the position of that percept in my perceptual field which I interpret as witnessing to your conscious existence and which I call your "body", what percepts you must be having. Once we recognise this, we are being as objective as is the naïve believer in objective "matter". The baby soon learns to distinguish percepts from images and memory-pictures, and he soon learns that his percepts are related to other people's percepts in a way that his images are not. To say that matter exists and to say that there are objective laws governing the relations between one another's perceptual fields comes to precisely the same thing in practice.

C

"But why, then, all the fuss?" someone may say. This is quite a fair question. Whether or not we insist that impersonal language can be adequately translated into personal language, whether or not we interpret language about matter as language about objective laws of perception, makes no difference in practice. We continue to help one another move the furniture and we play cricket together. But nevertheless the point is not mere logic-chopping. It is of an importance impossible to exaggerate. For language can be what Professor Ryle has called "systematically misleading". It can suggest to us quite unwarrantable metaphysical beliefs. Now, our everyday language, which is a quite uncritical mixture of personal and impersonal language, has suggested to us a quite groundless metaphysic. A suggestion conveyed to us by the structure of language can be both subtle and inescapable. It can foist off on to us as a fact what is really a dubious theory. But once we have seen that the popular, uncritical notion of "matter" is completely unnecessary—that we can adequately describe the universe without it —the philosophy of materialism collapses like a house of cards. The idea that the Universe started as a lot of bits of matter, out of all relation to mind, and that somehow this matter "produced" mind, is little more intellectually respectable than are the creation myths of the ancients.

A person can, of course, refuse to make the translation from impersonal to personal language. But the operative word is "refuse". He cannot deny that the translation can be made, and he is therefore deliberately choosing to affirm a dualism of consciousness and dead matter when he can perfectly well deal with the universe in terms of one type of entity only—conscious events.

"But why not?" someone may say. "Why may we not prefer a dualism, or even a pluralism if it comes to that?" The answer is that in no other department of thought do we prefer to affirm a dualism when we can reach a unity. The aim of the scientist —it is one of our most fundamental intellectual instincts—is to see his field as a systematic unity. The classic instance is the law of gravitation—Newton's or Einstein's. Once men see that it is possible to unify a vast mass of disparate data—to make a wide generalization which exhibits a lot of "apparently" different facts as One Fact—they plump for the One Fact as The Truth. It is rational to trust our instinct for unity. It operated in men's thinking long before they became explicitly aware of it; whatever gods or forces made us, made us think that way; when we think that way the Universe is, so to speak, thinking in us. Moreover, the trust in this instinct has been brilliantly vindicated all over the vast field of sciences.

But if we reject the alleged dualism of "mind" and "matter", we cannot rest in a sheer spiritual pluralism. Empirically, of course, the pluralism of consciousness is not absolute. My experiences and yours are obviously connected in *some* way. In *some* sense the Universe of consciousnesses is a Universe and not a sheer Multiverse. We begin to see a rational basis for the idea of God.

Our argument, then, comes to this. Language about "the material world" can be quite adequately interpreted as language about the perceptual experiences of conscious beings. We do not need the concept of a material world right "outside" us. In a sense our percepts are *in* us, although it is better to avoid the misleading spatial metaphor "in". We can put it another way. A person's percepts are part of *him*; a person is a continuum of perceptual, emotional and volitional experience. Scientific hypotheses and laws expressed in language about particles, or about the movements of so-called material objects, can be translated into hypotheses or laws relating some of a person's percepts to other of his percepts, or relating one person's percepts to another person's percepts. It would be inconvenient to carry on discussions in this translated language; indeed, everyday language and scientific language has evolved because of its practical convenience. But the fact that the translation *can* be made is of an importance impossible to exaggerate when we are starting philosophical construction.

For example, language about the effects of skull injuries,

brain operations, or drug injections, or people's conscious states, and the converse language about people's mental events or states causing physical changes in their bodies, has to be radically re-interpreted. Language about Mr. Brown's body is language about the way his existence, thoughts, and actions as a conscious being are represented by perceptual symbols in other people's perceptual fields. There are not two realms, a physical and a mental, between which causal laws operate. There is only one realm, and all scientific laws whatsoever are laws about connections between people's experiences. Instead of our thinking of a man as primarily a body, with mental events as a sort of functionless by-product, we see that man is primarily a spirit, and that laws stated in language about alleged physical objects, including bodily organisms, is elliptical language about men's percepts.

"But," someone may say, "this is fantastic. I am going to stick to my solid three-dimensional world—something simple that I can understand." But, unfortunately, while you are bowing the idealist philosopher out of the front door, the physicist is coming in at the back. You just *cannot* have your nice easily "understood" three-dimensional world, for the physicist is bringing with him one just as "fantastic" as the idealist philosopher's. I am referring, of course, to the Minkowski world associated with the Special Theory of Relativity.

"But," you may say, "the Special Theory of Relativity does not really challenge our belief in the three-dimensional world-in-itself. It introduces only a small modification in it. Indeed, for all practical purposes the Theory makes no difference; only if we were moving, relatively to one another, at speeds so vast that we never attain them, would our everyday picture of the material world prove incorrect."

The answer to this is that two very different meanings can be attached to the phrase "for practical purposes the Theory makes no difference". Let us consider this. First, let us suppose ourselves attending the annual business meeting of a tennis club. In discussing the budget for next season, the whole discussion proceeds, let us say, on the assumption that we have £30 in hand. Now suppose someone suddenly says "But that is incorrect; the balance is only £29 19s." We very reasonably reply that £30 is a near enough approximation; for practical purposes it makes no difference. But now suppose an aged widow, who has no head for business, is living on the interest from a small investment left by her husband. Let us further suppose that the company in which the money is invested goes bankrupt, with practically no assets, but that a wealthy friend tells the lady's solicitor to keep the news from her. "Send her a cheque each quarter as before, and recover from me."

Now in one respect our two illustrations are similar; in another respect they are quite different. They are similar in that in both cases we can use the expression "It makes no difference in practice." In the first case, to say "We have £30", although not quite accurate, is near enough for all practical purposes. In the second case, again, so far as the old lady is concerned it makes no difference whether the company is solvent or not; her sense-data—the cheque she sees and handles and the goods she buys with it—are the same in either case. But the two cases differ vastly in that in one of them it is the objective situation that is practically unaffected; £30 in the bank is almost the same as £29 19s.; but in the second case we have a totally different objective situation producing identical sense-data.

Now which of these two illustrations best fits the case of the Special Theory of Relativity? Anyone who knows enough mathematics to understand the Lorentz transformation will realize, when he reflects on the point, that the widow illustration fits the case far better than the tennis club illustration. The Minkowski world is, metaphysically, quite different from the Newtonian world. The fact that in normal circumstances we get the same sensory-cheques from either world and buy the same perceptual experiences ought not to be allowed to obscure the vast objective difference between the two worlds. We can extend our analogy further. We can imagine that contrary to all the probabilities, the old lady outlives the benefactor, and that the latter has not provided in his will for the payments to go on. In that event, the lady *would* notice the vast difference between what she had hitherto believed to be the objective situation and what it really was. Similarly, in the unlikely event of someone's travelling at a very vast velocity relatively to the earth, or having to make calculations in the field of atomic theory, his view of the objective situation might have to change radically.

From the standpoint of philosophy, then, the fact that only in rare circumstances does the relativity-picture have to be used, can in no wise soften the blow to anyone in love with the Newtonian picture. To keep harping on the theme that the objective situation appears to differ very little from the Newtonian picture is to emulate the girl in *Midshipman Easy* who excused the illegitimacy of her offspring on the ground that it was very little! The simple truth is that the old firm has gone out of business. There *are* no objective space dimensions, no objective time measurements; there is, indeed, no *matter*, unless we use this word with a quite new meaning. There is, indeed, objective physical *truth*; we cannot believe just what we like. But the *entities* are utterly different from what we used to think, and it is impossible to exaggerate the importance of the difference for philosophy, when, for example, we come to discuss the relation between thinkers and object of thought, or the so-called relation between soul and body.

But what, then, has Relativity put in place of the three-dimensional world-in-itself in a common objective time? The answer is that it has put nothing in its place except a set of equations—equations of "transformation". By using these equations one person can express another person's space and time measurements as functions of his own space and time measurements. In other words, the equations express the objective laws connecting our respective perceptual worlds. These equations are more complex than was believed in pre-relativity times; in particular, my measurements and your measurements of the time interval between what we call "the same pair of events" will not, in general, be the same, although only in rare circumstances will the difference be appreciable.

Now the truth of the foregoing has tended to be obscured by the fact that ingenious models can be devised which "illustrate" or "interpret" the equations. One simple model is the well-known "Minkowski World". This is a sort of picture of a four-dimensional "world" or continuum consisting of points of "space-time"; there are three space dimensions and one time dimension, and we carry out measurements along four lines all perpendicular to each other ("rectangular co-ordinates", as they are called).[1] But no competent physicist imagines that this model is a simple picture of a world-in-itself which is "out there". It no more "mirrors" the objective situation—the objective laws expressed by the equations of transformation—than a railway time-table stuck on a notice board, or a graph hanging at the railway headquarters, mirrors the actual trains running. For example, the ink marks on the time-table do not move; the trains do. In the same way the "Minkowski World" is static; by representing time as a "dimension" you freeze all motion. Moreover, you can have your four-dimensional model only by using "complex numbers", which, although quite logical, are very different from simple integers. One way of writing them, indeed, involves the use of a symbol for the square root of minus one. The whole business is nothing more than a useful mental device; anyone who believes the model "really exists in itself" must be capable of believing anything!

"But," some may say, "you have not produced a strict proof —a logically necessary proof—that a world-in-itself does not exist." Of course I have not, for the simple reason that one cannot, in *this* sense, prove the non-existence of any alleged entity whatsoever—a jabberwock or unicorn, for example. The burden of proof, or at least of evidence, for an existential statement is always on him who affirms it. When I say, "I see no reason to believe in matter because I can translate any impersonal sentence into a personal one", I am saying all that in the

[1] This simple model relates only to the *Special* Theory of Relativity.

nature of the case *can* be said. If you wish to refute me you must point to some perceptual situation in which such translation breaks down. You cannot do this.

But it is not only relativity that will bother you if you insist on your dead world-in-itself. There are also the findings of the atomic physicist. You talk of particles of matter, and a particle is, in ordinary language, something which has definite position and definite velocity. But the atomic physicist tells you that when he tries to deal with the fundamental, very tiny, particles of which at one time it seemed natural to suppose that an atom was composed—the electrons, for example—he finds that there are no such entities. If we try to think of a particle, we find that the more accurately we can find exactly where it is, the less accurately we can find at what velocity it is moving. And the more accurately we can find at what velocity it is moving, the less accurately we can discover where it is. And this does not merely mean that it *has* an exact position and an exact velocity but that we cannot ascertain these. It means, so we are assured, that it is nonsense to talk of its absolute position or velocity at all. But this means that it isn't really a particle at all, for a particle by definition has definite position and velocity.

The simple truth is that the modern physicist, when he is thinking about fundamentals, is forced to do precisely what the idealist philosopher says we ought to do before we begin on constructive philosophy—translate impersonal language into language about conscious beings and their experiences. When we read books on the philosophy of modern physics we find the writers continually referring to the observer, to our concepts, to our language. There are constant references to probability, to uncertainty, to potentiality. We can cast this language into objective form, but when we come to analyse it, we find ourselves referring to ourselves, our ignorance, the limits and the vagueness of our knowledge.

The attitude of scientists themselves towards all this is a little surprising—or would be unless we remembered that scientists are only human, after all. There are exceptions, of course, to any generalization, but on the whole it is fair to say that when not consciously attending to the fact that our whole conception of a three-dimensional world-in-itself has been revolutionized by the experimental discoveries which necessitated the Lorentz transformation and the Special Theory of Relativity, they drop back, like everyone else, into the pre-relativity way of thinking and talking about "matter". This is quite understandable. The relative velocities of the objects which biologists, for example, are studying are so small that, so far as pure biology is concerned, there is no need for them to think in terms of world-points and the four-dimensional continuum; the "common-sense" world is sufficient for their purpose. But when, as so often happens these days, they tend to leave pure biology and enter the fields of psychology and metaphysics, or discuss the so-called body-mind problem, then they ought to be acutely aware that the whole concept of a material world-in-itself has been undermined. The same criticism can be made of the cosmologists. Eddington was one of the few who really faced the idealist implications of modern physics.

The reason why those of us who insist on interpreting impersonal language in personal terms cannot be shown to be mistaken is that we are not putting forward a theory; we are, in taking this attitude, *refusing* to theorize. To say that people, with their respective perceptual fields, exist, is not to advance anything contentious. We *all* agree about this. If this belief can be called a theory, it is one to which we are committed by the very act of thinking at all. But to try to "explain" the obvious relatedness and inter-dependence of our respective perceptual fields by saying that there is a world-in-itself of dead matter, existing out of all relation to any mind whatsoever, man's or God's, is to engage in speculation which is neither verifiable nor falsifiable by any empirical observation whatsoever.

The passion for insisting that by "the real world" we mean something out of all relation to any mind whatsoever is curiously perverse. It could not, in the nature of things, have any empirical support, and it ignores the simple fact that the perceptual world which each of us experiences is closely integrated with the ego of each of us. If we carefully analyse the sentence "I perceive some moving objects" we find that what is symbolized by "I" and what is symbolized by the words "moving objects" are logically inter-dependent.[2]

But someone may say "There may be no verbal answer to your arguments. But there are certain experiences which give us a feeling that somehow you must be wrong. For example, we visit a cave, and the guide points out some stalagmites and stalactites. Are you denying that the process of forming these really did go on for vast ages in the dark, hidden from all observation?"

The answer is simple. Of course something *did* "go on", something objective. I am not suggesting that what the guide told you about the stalagmites was sheer imagination, as it would have been had he told you that they were made by fairies. I quarrel with you only if you pretend to have precise knowledge of alleged events "outside" or "independent of" all human awareness. For in the nature of things you cannot have such knowledge. To say that everything a man is perceiving would be happening, precisely as he perceives it, if he were not perceiving it, is to lay claim to know what you cannot know. For example, you indicate your belief that the stalagmite processes did go on "in the dark". But were the stalagmites coloured as they are now that you see them? Can there be colours when no one is seeing colours, smells when no one is smelling, sounds when no one is hearing, pressures when no one is feeling pressed? "Granted," you may say, "but these are secondary qualities. The primary qualities—like position and shape and motion—*they* are objective." But consider. How is a position, a shape, a motion, defined for you? Only by those secondary qualities which you have agreed to exist as mental objects only. The only shape you have ever experienced has been a seen or a

---

[2] A reader who wishes to consider this point more thoroughly will find it set out on pages 32–42 of my book *Christian Rationalism and Philosophical Analysis*. James Clarke, 1959.

felt shape. The line, the edge, was defined by a sharp colour-separation, or by a touch-feeling. The alleged "primary" qualities, qualities which you claim to be objective, seem inextricably involved in the "secondary" qualities which you admit are mental objects only.

The simple truth is that all we can claim to know about the stalagmites is that the general objective situation, for which we use the term "Reality", was such that finite intelligences with our mental faculties could, if the required conditions had been fulfilled, have perceived the growth of stalagmites.

Similarly with all language about the material world. In the *Radio Times* of September 28, 1961, a notice about a broadcast talk tells us that we have now come to know that the proton and the neutron are revealed not as simple points but as little spheres containing electric charges and currents. Am I denying, or in any way challenging, what is here written? Not in the least. I am only offering the most cautious philosophical analysis of the language, the interpretation which confines itself to that minimum metaphysical construction which we *are* forced to make, and declined to indulge in unnecessary constructions.[3] What are the facts which we *must* admit? That certain scientists exist, who have had certain perceptual experiences which they explain or account for by certain mathematical calculations which they illustrate or interpret by mental pictures of protons or neutrons. They regard their mathematical equations as valid in the sense that they are verified, or at least not falsified, by perceptual observations. These are statements about *persons* and their experiences and mental activities. So far as science and everyday life are concerned there is no *need* for me to raise any further questions. I am in no way obliged to raise the question, "What sort of further reality have I to postulate in order to account for the existence of the persons and their percepts?"

But if I choose to raise this question, as I have every right to,

---

[3] What I mean by this is that even to talk about people having percepts is to make a metaphysical construction.

then I ought to face the fact that I am indulging in metaphysical speculation. The notion that there is a dead material world-in-itself is an extremely speculative metaphysical construction. People who object to talk about "God" on the ground that this is unverifiable metaphysics must face the fact that talk about self-existent "matter" is also unverifiable metaphysics. Either we admit metaphysics or we do not. If we do not, belief in matter is as untenable as theism. If we do, then I shall argue that a far stronger case can be made out for theism than for a belief in a dead world-in-itself.

I have already indicated that no one can dispense with metaphysics altogether. For the belief that persons—that conscious beings—exist is a metaphysical belief. Solipsism, the belief that I alone exist, cannot be refuted by logically necessary argument; a solipsist cannot be convicted of self-contradiction. Nor can his thesis be falsified by any experience whatsoever, for he can interpret any experience solipsistically. To believe that a universe of persons with their respective perceptual worlds exists is, therefore, a metaphysical hypothesis. One is, therefore, being inconsistent if one objects to speculating as to what is "behind" our percepts—asking how best to account for our perceptual experience and the fact that my and your experiences are closely inter-related.

But anyone who has followed my argument will see that although we are justified in postulating some Reality to which all true impersonal statements, including scientific statements, in some way "correspond" and to which imaginings and false statements do not correspond, nevertheless we have no right to claim that this Reality is obviously a dead material world-in-itself. On the contrary, since impersonal language can be translated into personal language, and can be regarded as elliptical ways of talking about actual and possible experiences, there are clearly very strong grounds for regarding Reality as more akin to subject-with-object than as dead abstract object. What is "behind" the veil of sense-data and percepts is more appropriately thought of as *He* rather than *It*.

I can here imagine someone saying "It is now clear that the driving-force behind this construction you have been offering us is a desire to vindicate Theism. But surely there are plenty of philosophers and theologians who believe in God but who do not call themselves 'idealists'—who never attack the notion of a material world-in-itself. Was it really necessary to try to approach belief in God in the way that you have done?"

My answer would be that there are, of course, other lines of approach. I shall, indeed, be indicating another such line in the next chapter. But one thing seems certain, and I have never met a theist who was prepared to challenge me on the point; a theist cannot consistently believe in a world-in-itself out of all relation to all Mind whatsoever. He must think of God as, by definition, all-knowing; he cannot think of God as ignorant, or as being, like us, unable to attend to too many things at one time so that they, as it were, fall into His "sub-conscious". That would be far too crude an anthropomorphism! By definition, all God's awareness is completely explicit. The question, there-fore, of a world-in-itself existing out of all relation to a Mind simply does not arise for the theist. In the only sense in which I declare myself an idealist, *every* consistent theist must be an idealist.

There exists, then, the world-for-Jones—the world as Jones perceives it—or, more accurately, Jones-with-his-world. Similarly with Brown and Robinson, you and me. When we ask, "What must be postulate to account for all these?" the answer is, "The world-for-God, or God-with-all-that-He-is-aware-of." When we say, "The world as Jones perceives it has such and such features, while the world as Brown perceives it has slightly different or greatly different features; what is it *really*?" we do not mean, or we ought not to mean, "What is it *in itself*?" but, "What is it *for God*?"

The view I am advocating has nothing whatever in common with statements by exponents of certain Oriental religions to the effect that the material world "does not exist" or is "an illusion", or with the Christian heresies which regarded matter as essentially evil. My exposition has been a clarification, in twentieth-century language, of the essential insight of the eighteenth-century Bishop Berkeley who had, in many respects, a typically down-to-earth Western mind, besides being an orthodox Christian. It is absurd to say "the material world does not exist". The question at issue is merely that of the correct analysis of the true statement that it does exist. The hard-headed early Victorian empiricists who defined "matter" as "the permanent possibility of sensation"—and T. H. Huxley seems to have agreed with them—were as far from Oriental mysticism as is any materialist.

The Western view is here, I believe, correct. It is absurd to try to dismiss as "illusion" whatever we do not happen to approve of. And it is absurd to call matter "evil". The noblest thoughts and resolves have their nerve-correlates just as do the basest.

Now in this chapter I shall not carry this argument farther. I shall pursue it in Chapter 6. At this point I can only hope that I have convinced the reader that it is easier to reduce the material to the mental than the mental to the material, that the Universe is in some sense a unitary system, and that this is some indication of the rationality of a faith in God which most believers reach by some kind of intuitive certainty anyway.

The simple truth is, of course, that an argument for belief in God reached solely by an analysis of the nature of perception gives us far less than is needed for vital religion. The bare conception of God as the Mind in whom finite minds exist—the thesis that what is "behind" our percepts must be referred to as "He" rather than "It"—is quite insufficient. But the fact that a concept is insufficient does not prove that it is not necessary. To say "He" rather than "It" does not seem of great importance in itself, but it is impossible to exaggerate its importance as opening the door to boundless possibilities which are shut if we cannot, in this bare sense, say "He". If you say "It" when speaking of what is "behind" our experience, you are logically bound to give a totally different interpretation of a whole range of human experiences—those which distinguish men from animals—those which we term moral and æsthetic and spiritual—from the explanation which we can give if we say "He". To say "It" means that we have to try to explain man from below upwards—to explain human evolution by its beginnings, not its consummation; we have the hopeless task of trying to explain man as a super-ape evolved by chance or by blind law. This means that we cannot explain, but must explain *away*, everything distinctly human. But to say "He" means that we can see the evolutionary process as having purpose, and we interpret its meaning not by its beginnings, its biological origins, but by its highest achievements. We look not for a biological but a theological explanation of spirituality and morality. We regard everything as revealing God in *some* measure, but man at his best as revealing God in the highest measure we can bear. That is part of the truth of the Christian doctrine of the Incarnation.

The crucial problem facing the moral philosopher is the problem whether on the one hand our beliefs about right and wrong are merely matters of individual taste—expressions of purely subjective emotions—or whether they correspond to something in the Scheme of Things. Is the man who holds on to his integrity against strong temptation asserting a defiant and desperate morality against a reality which is at best indifferent and at worst hostile? Or, on the contrary, is conscience an *insight* into an objectively moral order—as objective, in its way, as is the mathematical order in *its* way? From the time when men first began to speculate on the deeper meaning of life, there have been those who, far from trying to explain our moral consciousness, have tried to explain it away. In Plato's *Republic*, one of the characters in the dialogue argues that the notion of justice is merely a device of the weak to curb the strong; cunning is being matched against power. Now it is clear that if the case for objective morality is to be maintained against those who would explain it away as a cunning device or as merely a matter of individual taste, it is vital that we should be able to appeal to considerations outside the sphere of ethics which show that reality is of such a nature that it can, so to speak, *house* objective moral values. If the ultimate realities are conceived as *impersonal* forces or entities, then we shall have to admit that there is no more question of the sadist being objectively wrong and the humanitarian objectively right than there is of the man who prefers tea for breakfast being objectively wrong and the man who prefers coffee being objectively right. It is all merely a question of individual taste; reality, like Gallio, cares for none of these things. You can, of course, get keen on advocating honesty or kindliness, just as you can get keen on recommending some brand of coffee!

But if, on the other hand, we refuse thus to ridicule the deep conviction of good men and women all down the ages that the moral conscience somehow corresponds to or expresses something in the heart of reality, then we must admit that reality must be of such a nature as can house or hold morality; indeed, reality must at bottom, be moral. But the impersonal cannot be moral. It follows, then, that an objective view of the moral conscience is not merely consistent with, but demands, the truth of our purely metaphysical argument for God.

Similar considerations apply, of course, to values other than the moral values. When we listen to the Hallelujah Chorus, or to the setting of "Praise to the Holiest" in Elgar's *Dream of Gerontius*, we have a deep conviction that our state of mind is not merely emotional but is somehow a flash of insight This conviction must be explained away, and the whole thing debunked, if we hold that man is the highest intelligence in the Universe. We can, then, claim with confidence that our analysis of Reality as basically mental is completely in harmony with our moral and spiritual experience. "He" who is the source of all being is also the source of all good and all beauty.

And one thing is luminously clear—the choice is between believing in God and debunking man.

CHAPTER 3

The Relation between Religion and Conduct

IN THE latter part of Chapter 2 we were approaching a subject on which a great deal has been written by philosophers in recent years, namely, the connection between metaphysics and ethics. There are philosophers who deny that there *is* any connection, and this denial is but the academic equivalent to the notion, popular in certain circles, that there is no connection between religious faith and living a good life. This notion is derived, with ludicrous light-heartedness, from the fact that some quite nice people do not go to church.

It needs, of course, much more careful consideration, for these nice people have clearly been influenced by the ethics of the society in which they were born, and human societies have never kept their religion and their morals in separate compartments.

Those who deny connection between metaphysics and ethics reason as follows. There is no way, they say, of arguing from facts to values or to moral obligations. We must therefore study ethics, or moral philosophy, in complete disregard of our metaphysical views as to the nature of things. Let us consider this.

When we say that we cannot draw ethical conclusions from metaphysical facts, we mean that no statement of the form "S is P" can possibly entail any statement of the form "It is our duty to do so-and-so". Now someone may at once reply that this is nonsense, for if, for example, we make the statement "The people at such-and-such a place are short of food", we go on to draw the inference, "We ought to send them food". We

D

are clearly drawing an ethical inference from a factual statement; we are arguing from a fact to an obligation.

But this objection has missed the point. When we say that n
factual statement can possibly entail a statement of moral obl
gation, the important word is "entail". Philosophers and log
cians usually use this word with great precision. To say that or
statement entails another means that if you affirm the first an
deny the second you fall into *self-contradiction*. Entailment
that special form of inference which we meet in the study
Euclid. It is a process of argument in which the conclusions ar
shown to be entirely latent within the premises. That is wh
Immanuel Kant called the statement of an entailment an anal
tical statement.

Now once we are clear on this point, we can see that it
perfectly true that no statement of fact can *entail* a statemer
of moral obligation. To say that people are hungry does no
contain within itself, ready to be drawn out, as it were, by
process of pure logic, the statement that we ought to send the
food. But to say that there is no logical entailment between th
two statements is one thing; to say that there is no sort of co
nection between them would be quite another, and absurd. T
say that people are hungry does somehow *evoke* the statemer
that we ought to send them food. In short, factual statement
including those general statements about the Scheme of Thing
which we call metaphysical statements, may not *entail* state
ments of moral obligation, but to deny all connection betwee
metaphysics and ethics is absurd. The curious thing is that th
very philosophers who wish to cut off ethics entirely fro
metaphysics usually insist that ethical sentences are expressio
of the emotional and volitional sides of our nature, not of th
cognitive side. Now, the connection between what we cogniz
or think we cognize, and our emotional and practical reaction
is obvious. If I think I see a tiger coming down the street m
emotions are aroused and I am spurred to activity. In the sam
way it would be silly to deny that my metaphysical beliefs, m
beliefs about the nature of things (belief, for instance, in Go

as revealed in Jesus), may evoke emotional and practical reactions, of the kind which are called "good" in everyday language.

But we must be fair. In denying that facts entail obligations the philosophers are making a valid, and, indeed, an important point. In saying that the strictly moral "I ought" cannot be simply deduced from any statement of fact, they had in mind two examples. First, there were theologians who sometimes talked as though our obligation to obey moral law was *entailed* by the statement that there is a good God. When Immanuel Kant challenged this, he was very far from denying the existence of a good God. His point was that, although in the order of Being, so to speak, God comes first, yet in the order of our knowing, the moral law comes first. If we start with belief in a good God, and then say "Therefore I must obey His laws", we *may* not be moral at all. We may be moved by fear or by enlightened self-interest. He argued in the reverse direction. It is because we have this mysterious something within us which leads us to the conviction that we ought to do so-and-so even if there is no reward to be gained and no punishment to be feared —it is because of *this* that we can believe that the Author of our being is good. Kant agreed that the obligation to be moral is not entailed by the statement that God exists; but he also held that belief that God exists is implied, although not entailed, by belief in moral obligation.

It is important here to guard against a misunderstanding. It might be thought that if acceptance of moral obligation is a sort of premise from which belief in God is drawn as a conclusion, then people's practical moral reactions will be the same whether they explicitly draw the theistic conclusion or not. But every student of logic knows that if one proposition implies another, then doubt or denial of what is implied implies doubt or denial of the premise. If the categorical imperative implies theism, then atheism implies denial of the categorical imperative. Objective implication, of course, is one thing; whether people draw the inference is another. But in the long run logic will out. Rational self-conscious beings cannot be expected to give a blind obedience to an alleged imperative which they cannot fit into their view of the nature of things, which they cannot see as integrated into a coherent metaphysic. If they have to think of the categorical imperative as a brute fact bearing no relation to the scheme of things, they have every right to doubt whether there *is* a categorical imperative. We must either see the existence of objective moral obligation as the key to the mystery of life, or we must doubt whether there is any objective moral obligation.

While, therefore, moral philosophers are right in holding that moral obligation cannot be explained as, or reduced to, fear of God's wrath or a desire to win His favour, it does not follow that there is no connection between acceptance of moral obligation and belief in God.

In denying that facts can logically entail moral obligations, philosophers often have in mind an argument not of theologians but of certain scientists. This argument is usually referred to as the argument for evolutionary ethics. These scientists have drawn certain very broad conclusions as to the course of biological evolution—the kinds of human beings and human situations which it seems actually to be tending to produce—and from these purely factual statements they go on to say, in effect, "Therefore we ought to behave in accordance with these evolutionary trends". Now it is only necessary to bring this argument out into clear daylight to see its fallacy. The fact that evolution has, in fact, tended in certain directions in the past is completely irrelevant in considering the question what ought we now to do. On the principle of natural selection alone, without going into philosophy, it would seem that our power to criticize and, if necessary, to oppose previous trends would never have been selected unless it had some survival value. In any case we have every right to see the utmost possible significance in the fact that evolution has produced beings who *have* the power to reverse the trends of evolution, beings who revolt against the suggestion that they are only super-apes and must behave like super-apes. In short, no evolutionary fact can be allowed to weigh against a moral conviction.

But, as we have seen, to say that the theologian's statements about God and the biologist's statements about evolution do not logically entail ethical doctrines, is one thing. To say that beliefs about God or about evolution cannot affect our theories of ethics and our practical moral reactions, would be quite another. Let us now examine the question in a little more detail.

In the study of ethics or moral philosophy we have, I believe, to study three distinct, although connected, topics. First, there is the question of the *meaning* of statements about moral obligation. What do I really mean, or what should I mean if I were clear-headed, when I say that I ought, or that it is my duty, or that it is right, to do so-and-so, or that it would be wrong to do it, or my duty not to do it, or that I ought not to do it? The second question is that of the moral criterion. How do we decide what is right and what is wrong? The third is the practical question of the moral incentive. How can we get people to be good and do good?

First, the question of the meaning of statements about moral obligation. Broadly speaking, we have to distinguish two schools of thought—those who believe that statements about right and wrong are objective, and those, on the contrary, who believe that they are merely subjective. As an example of an objective statement consider the sentence "All swans are entirely white". Now if someone replies "No. Some swans are not entirely white", then you have a strict contradiction; one of the statements must be true and the other false, since both swans and white objects exist and the statements purport to state facts. But if someone says "China tea is nicer than Indian tea", and then someone else says "No. Indian tea is nicer", you do not have a contradiction at all. It is true that *in form*, both statements purport to be factual; *in form*, an objective quality of niceness is predicated of tea and, in form, therefore, we have a strict contradiction. But actually, of course, there is no contradiction, for when someone says that Indian tea is nicer than China tea this is only an elliptical way of saying that he personally prefers Indian tea. There is no contradiction involved in the fact that Smith prefers Indian and that Brown prefers China tea. Now, moral judgments, such as "Telling lies is wrong", "One ought not to be cruel", are *in form* objective statements. But the question arises are they also *in substance* objective, like the statements about swans, or are they *in substance* subjective, like the statements about tea? When I say "Cruelty is wrong", am I *merely* giving vent to my feelings, expressing my emotions, taking up a practical attitude towards cruelty and steeling myself to do something about it? I *am*, of course, often doing these things when I express moral judgments, but is this all there is to it? Am I not *also* making a factual statement which must, therefore, be either correct or incorrect according as it agrees with or disagrees with some fact outside the field of human likes and dislikes?

Now if I take the subjective view of morals, then I hold that when one man says that telling lies, or polygamy, is right and another says these are wrong, then they are not contradicting each other; they are merely expressing preferences, rooted in the emotional and volitional sides of their natures. There is no question, as there was in the case of the white swans, of one being correct and the other incorrect; the case is analogous to that of preferences for different brands of tea. But if I take the objective view, I can consistently hold that even if all living people think telling lies or being cruel is right, this makes no difference to the objective fact that lying and cruelty are wrong. These people are as incorrect as if they stated that large doses of arsenic are good for the baby.

Now my own view on the point at issue is that in one respect moral judgments are like statements about the niceness of China tea. I think moral judgments are rooted in our *feelings*. I do not believe that a conscious being capable of logic and mathematics, but incapable of emotions, would be capable of moral judgments. But on the other hand I cannot dismiss as an illusion that universal conviction that in *some* sense moral judgments have objective validity, and I do not believe that a high morality would ever have been attained unless human beings had had this belief. Broadly speaking, the more intensely people feel about morals, the more sure they are that somehow—explain it as we can—ethical statements express more than merely human desires; in this respect they are *not* like statements about the niceness of tea but are like statements about the colour of swans; they can be correct or incorrect. We feel that in some sense all values, moral and æsthetic, are objective. A person who approves of lying, or rejoices in cruelty, or prefers the music of rock-and-roll to that of Bach, is as much in conflict with something objective as is Brown minor when he thinks that three sevens make twenty-five.

Now I do not think that the point at issue can be decided by that intellectual discipline which, in recent years, we have called philosophical analysis. Our decision must turn, surely, on our metaphysical beliefs. Those modern philosophers who, following C. L. Stevenson, claim that moral statements *merely* express human attitudes or emotions and are not, therefore, strictly speaking statements at all—these philosophers are dominated, although many of them would not admit it, by an implicit metaphysical theory of reality. They are sure that ethical judgments cannot be objective because they assume objective reality to be of such a nature as could not, so to speak, *house* objective valuations. If it were possible to accept the thesis that man is the highest intelligence there is, somehow produced by impersonal basic entities or forces—material particles, bundles of energy, logical atoms, or sensa—then all talk about objective values, any suggestion that values inhere in anything independent of individual preferences, would surely be meaningless. It is fair to suspect that those philosophers who are sure that ethical judgments cannot be objective are influenced by some such metaphysics. But most people who feel strongly on moral issues will be more sure that moral values are objective than of the truth of any metaphysical systems which conflict with such objectivity. In short, instead of rejecting ethical objectivity because it does not square with some particular metaphysical theory, we have every right to reject any metaphysical theory which cannot square with ethical objectivity. But it is impossible to make any sense of the notion of cosmic ethical objectivity without postulating cosmic moral purpose, and it is impossible to make sense of the notion of cosmic moral purpose without postulating something analogous to Objective Mind.

Before I leave this question of moral objectivity, I must point out, in passing, that this question is quite distinct from one which I find is often confused with it, namely the question whether there are any moral rules to which there are no exceptions. There is a number of very general statements of what moral philosophers have called *prima facie* moral obligations, such, for instance, as that we must not tell lies, or that we must keep our promises, or that we must not hurt people's feelings. The vast majority of moral situations which confront us in our daily lives are resolvable by the simple application of one of these general rules, but occasionally the rules conflict. To tell the truth may hurt someone's feelings; to refuse to deceive a bandit may permit him to do untold harm, and so on. It is because of these moral conflicts that morality is a matter of the use of reason, and not of a blind obedience to laws. It would seem, indeed, that the only rules which one can say must *always* be followed must be so general, so vague, as to be useless in particular crises. To say that one should always aim at increasing human well-being is unexceptionable, but can hardly solve any real moral dilemma.

Now the fact that moral rules have to be thought about, and weighed one against the other—the fact that there are few moral rules to which, in exceptional circumstances, exceptions will not have to be made—has nothing to do with the question of moral objectivity. For we can still quite consistently maintain that although each particular moral situation must be considered on its merits, there nevertheless is always one solution which is the right one—the one which God would approve in those special circumstances.

There is another confusion of which we must beware. It is sometimes said that morality cannot be objective because people differ about right and wrong. This is like saying that arithmetic cannot be objective because students may give different answers to a calculation, or that meteorology cannot be objective because some affirm and others deny that the moon affects the weather. Moreover, people who argue thus usually exaggerate the mount of moral disagreement in the world. On the broad fundamentals there is wide and deep agreement. All the great religions inculcate justice, mercy and truth. Even though marriage customs may differ there is universal agreement that sex needs hedging round with rigid rules.

I have said enough to show that the first of the three tasks of the moral philosopher—the elucidation of the notion of objective moral obligation—involves him in the consideration of metaphysics in general and theism in particular. It will be convenient to take the third task next. This is the least academic of the three; it is the challenge to the parent, the teacher, the welfare officer, the probation officer, the clergyman. It is the task set us by the intelligent young delinquent who asks defiantly, "Why *should* I do what you call right?" I am not now so much concerned with what it would be wise to say, on the spur of the moment, to the youth who thus confronted us. That would depend on our knowledge of the particular youth; we might even, in his case, be too late. I am concerned rather with the task of preventing young people getting into the state of mind when they defiantly ask such a question. We want them to get so keen on doing right that they would not dream of asking why *should* they do right.

Now, in the long run, the emotional attitude of people towards the moral law must depend on what they believe the moral law to be. If we take a long view, we must see that there will be no more potent factor for the creation or the killing of moral incentives than our answer to the question, "What is moral obligation?" This, we saw, depended on metaphysics. I believe that however irrelevant to morality one's ideas of the nature of things may be on a short view, they have the greatest possible relevance on a long view. I must deal with this in a little more detail.

It has been much emphasized of late in certain quarters that the average individual's moral opinions and reactions are determined not by the acceptance of any theory of morals but by the training and influences to which he has been subjected during childhood and adolescence, or, if you prefer it, by the way his reflexes have been conditioned. This is true, but let us also remember that human beings are capable of achieving a large measure of self-awareness. And the more intelligent ones, those who will lead and influence their fellows, will reach the stage when they will become explicitly aware that their whole system of moral sentiments is what it is because society has been conditioning their reflexes. When that moment is reached, they will be free either to acquiesce in, or else to revolt against, the intentions of those who have been conditioning them. Now, if a thoughtful young person comes to believe that his moral convictions are *nothing more than* the result of society's efforts to get him to subordinate his interests to society's interests, he may well feel no emotional urge to comply. It would be useless to tell him that he *ought* to comply, for *for him* words like "ought", "right" and "wrong" have been de-bunked. Plato saw the point long ago. He makes a character in one of his dialogues argue that the propagation of the notion of justice is merely a clever device of the weak to restrain the strong; cunning is being matched against strength; to propagate morality is to propagate superstition.

It is, I think, probably true that most people's moral convictions and habits are largely a matter of conditioned reflexes, and that they will continue in the moral habits they learned in childhood, at any rate if not tempted too strongly, without asking whether their uncritical ethical views fit their uncritical metaphysical views. But the more intelligent *will* ask this question, and will ask it more and more as self-awareness increases. I cannot believe that the conclusions they reach about the Source of moral obligation will not affect their conduct.

This point is so important that I must linger over it for a moment. Let us consider the ethical theory that regards morality entirely as a matter of human emotions and volitions. My conviction that a certain course of action is right corresponds to nothing outside the field of human valuations. Whatever gods or forces produced me are entirely indifferent to morals, and are not in the least concerned to vindicate the righteous. Now if this is true, the man who clings to his integrity, and does what he believes to be the right thing in the face of every inducement not to, is asserting a defiant and desperate morality in the face of a non-moral reality. I am not concerned at the moment to say that such a view is impossible or absurd, although, in passing, one can say that the very existence of human morality in such a Universe is an insoluble puzzle. I am merely making the point that such a view can hardly fail to be a discouragement to virtue. If the ultimate reality which produced me is non-moral, if there is no objective moral purpose in the Scheme of Things, human morality seems to be an ontological freak. To admit this must surely damp moral enthusiasm.

But surely we can go farther. To characterize such a Universe as non-moral seems an understatement. A Universe in which the destinies of finite consciousnesses with vast capacity for joy and suffering are finally at the mercy of non-moral forces can fairly be described as an evil Universe. One's decision as to the truth or falsity of such a view can hardly be irrelevant to moral motive.

But here I must consider an objection. I stated earlier that morality must stand on its own feet. For an action to be truly moral it must be done from the conviction that it ought to be done. If I do it merely to win reward or avoid punishment it is not a moral action at all. But now I am saying that if I believe the Scheme of Things to be so indifferent to virtue as to fail to vindicate the good, such a belief will diminish my moral enthu siasm. Is there not a contradiction here?

Now if you are going to insist that there is a contradiction you must follow your argument to its logical conclusion. You will have to say that the only person who can be strictly moral is one who does not believe his virtue will add to his happiness either in this life or in a hereafter. Morality, in short, must be essentially pessimistic. Now no one really believes this.

Actually, there is no contradiction. People do not act from just one motive. The pure moral motive *is* a factor in determin ing our actions, but its moral character is not destroyed if it is accompanied by a conviction that in a Universe which makes sense the good man must ultimately be vindicated—if not in this life then in the hereafter.

Each one of us must look into his own heart. I admit that if I were convinced that my sense of moral obligation was an in explicable brute fact in a non-moral scheme of things, my moral life would suffer. My personal feeling is that the moral impera tive cannot breathe for long in a religious vacuum. Unless I regard the moral urge as the key to the meaning of life, and thus come to believe in cosmic moral purpose, i.e. in God, my reverence for goodness will weaken. I cannot reverence it if I think of it as merely a human device for keeping society going.

An empirical study of the relation between religious belief and morals involves one in considerable complexity. An indi vidual, or a society, whose ethical habits have been conditioned by a culture in which religion has in the past played an impor tant part, does not alter its moral habits immediately when it changes its religious views. Inertia is a great force in human conduct. It is absurd to point to good English agnostics as prov ing that moral conduct is unconnected with religious faith. It is at least arguable that for the exhibition of a purely "natural" human ethic, uninfluenced by any of the great religions, we must look to Hitler and Stalin. It can at least be said that their attitude to their fellows was perfectly consistent with their rejection of the Christian doctrine of man.

There can be innumerable temporary substitutes for the fundamental moral motive—belief in God. One, as we have just noticed, is habit or inertia. There is a momentum in Christian ethics which operates after the dynamic of faith has been removed—but for how long? Or again, an individual with an unfortunate early experience of Christianity may express his hostility to it by an implicit, or even an explicit, determination to demonstrate that Christian ethics can be lived without the Christian creed. If Christianity died out, this motive would cease to operate, but that it is operating in Great Britain today one can hardly doubt.

We now come to the question of the moral criterion, the question of the tests to be applied to decide what actions are right and what wrong. One important test about which all theories agree is the way an action would tend to tip the balance between human happiness and human misery. Now, in popular discussions about politics or sociology it seems to be generally agreed that for a favourable balance of human happiness to be reached, the first thing to do is to ensure the continuance of the race. "Our very existence depends on. . . . " Any action tending to preserve the race is right; any action tending to destroy it would be wrong.

Now I am not disputing this; I merely point out that it is true only from the standpoint of an optimistic metaphysic. If the object of the good action is to secure a balance of happiness over misery, and prevent a balance of misery over happiness, then the question whether we ought to perpetuate the human race will depend on whether we believe that a permanent excess of happiness is not only possible but likely. The thing that amazes me is that so many people cheerfully hold this last belief while professing to hold a metaphysical world-view which provides not the slightest ground for it. If we cannot believe in an objective cosmic moral purpose, if we believe that human beings, with their vast capacity for suffering, have been produced by, and are at the mercy of, non-moral forces, then I cannot see anything morally axiomatic in the idea that we ought to seek to prolong the life of the race. If by pressing a button he could painlessly exterminate the race, a really rational and humane atheist might well feel strongly disposed to do so. And, if there is no objective cosmic purpose, it is futile to say "he ought not to!" For on that hypothesis your "ought" merely expresses your *own* feelings. But if, on the other hand, one believes in God and therefore in objective cosmic moral purpose, one will consistently refuse to press the button. One will feel that such vast issues must be left in His hands.

But we must consider further the nature of the moral criterion. It clearly derives from our natures as rational beings. It is no mere coincidence that human beings, who are capable, as animals are not, of arriving, with the aid of language, at the level of conceptual thought, should also be capable, as animals are not, of distinguishing some actions as right from others as wrong.

Human beings arrive at self-consciousness—a stage beyond the purely objective consciousness of the animals—because they can think conceptually. I am capable of explicitly noticing what I have in common with some beings and in what I differ from others. I then say "I belong to the class *human beings*." Now, once this stage had been reached, men could, and ultimately did, envisage the *possibility* of being just and impartial— of treating others as one would wish them to treat oneself, even if the translation of this possibility into actuality involved the negation of one's natural desires. But to envisage a possibility of action is not to desire to act accordingly. It is therefore a quite distinct fact (and we should deem it an amazing fact had we not become accustomed to it) that men not only conceived the possibility of negating their natural desires but actually felt an inward urge—however weak and impotent at first— to do so.

Now this suggests a very general criterion of moral action. It can be conceived as the kind of action open to us because of, and only because of our essentially human, rational nature. Broadly speaking, to do right and eschew evil is to be true to one's human nature in so far as this is other than our animal nature. This takes in at once the Greek ideal of sowing to the spirit rather than to the flesh, and the Roman ideal of justice. And since human beings are endowed with free imagination, we can conceive the possibility of going beyond mere justice, of being altruistic at the cost of self-sacrifice. (We must here remind ourselves that we are considering only the criterion— the awareness of moral possibilities. The moral motive, as we have seen, is quite another matter.)

So far we have been concerned with right actions. But not only are men capable of right actions; they can reflect on this fact. This complicates the situation. The emphasis swings from what I ought to do to the ideal man I ought to become. And the area of morally compulsive action is thereby greatly extended. The good man will feel that he ought not merely to want others to be happy but that he ought to want them to be good. In his reading of history he will tend to be more interested in it as a moral drama than in any other aspect—without, of course, necessarily losing his interest in these other aspects. He will feel the fact of moral values and moral conflict to be the key to the meaning of human life.

We have now arrived at the point when we are asking not merely what it is one's duty to do but what a really good person will *naturally* (in accordance with his *nature* as good) feel passionately concerned about. And I have not used lightly the word "passionately". Seeley was right when he wrote "No heart is pure that is not passionate; no virtue is safe that is not enthusiastic!"

Now one thing seems to me quite incontrovertible. A really good man will, above all things, long to be able to believe that behind the veil of sense, behind the realm of appearances, there is cosmic moral purpose. His whole soul will revolt against the suggestion that it is futile to want to see moral purpose in the Universe. He will *want* to believe in such purpose—partly for his own comfort and partly because such a belief is obviously a strong moral incentive and its rejection such an obvious moral discouragement, not only for himself but for others.

Now, to want to believe something is one thing; to feel one can and must believe it is quite another. And since genuine goodness includes honesty, the good man will be acutely aware of the difference. His awareness of his own bias will make it harder, not easier, for him to believe what he wants to. Every honest seeker after God knows how he is dogged by the thought "Is this just wishful thinking?" But on the other hand it would be silly for me to see in the fact that I want to believe something a positive reason for *not* believing it. Indeed, one can honestly go farther. The fact that the evolutionary process has produced beings who have this intense reverence for moral values, this deep-seated desire to see moral purpose in the Universe—this fact, surely, is a datum for philosophical construction of an importance impossible to exaggerate—far more significant than anything that physics or biology has to show.

Now it is vital to remember that the process of coming to believe in objective moral purpose, which ultimately means to believe in God—is not a matter of conducting a deductive or logically necessary argument. It is a construction, in the sense explained on page 25. In such a construction, one's honesty is tested not only by one's willingness to make one's arguments conform to the canons of inductive reasoning, as set forth, for example, in Mill's *Logic*, but also by one's willingness to search diligently for *all* the relevant data.

The good man will, therefore, make the search for such data one of the main objects of his life. He will face the fact that he cannot, and that he ought not to try to, believe beyond the evidence, but he will never give up the search for convincing evidence. Still less will he go around shouting his doubts and difficulties. It will be a sure sign of moral defect if he even subconsciously or unconsciously shies away from considerations pointing to ethical theism.

I am well aware that this argument appears to twist an academic discussion into a personal attack. But I honestly do not see how anyone who believes in God can consistently regard

belief in God as a purely intellectual affair like belief in a Euclidian proof. If there is a good God, He will not have so contrived
it that the essential qualification for arriving at faith in Him is
mere cleverness. This is not only common sense; it is the teaching of Scripture. To the upright there arises light in the darkness; it is the pure in heart who see God; if any man wills to do
His will, he shall know of the teaching whether it be of God.
This seems to mean not only that the good man will explicitly
seek for, and find, evidence which is available to all men as
such, but that he may have a type of evidence—spiritual experience—which no one can have who is not seeking God. There
is not, therefore, the slightest contradiction between the statement that we ought not to believe what is unreasonable or unevidenced, and the statement that the issue between belief and
unbelief in God is, at bottom, a moral one.

Does this imply moral censure of agnostics? Not necessarily
censure of any particular agnostic. The process whereby an
individual's character is formed is complex; early environment
and training count for a lot. Moreover, we cannot exhaustively
divide men into two classes—those whose intellectual integrity
is complete on the one hand and those who are consciously dis-
honest on the other. Few people would fall into either class;
few of us could claim that a wish-to-believe or a wish-to-deny
has not sometimes influenced the focussing of our attention.
Christians must always remember our Lord's "Judge not". But
truth must be served. When one is discussing these great issues
with anyone, it is usually quite easy to sense his bias. I do not
believe that it is possible to be emotionally detached where
consideration of Kant's great triad—God, moral freedom and
immortality—is concerned.

It is curious that my rational analysis of the moral consciousness has led me to much the same conclusion as theologians
who profess either to eschew rationalism, as is the case with
the existentialists, or else to eschew philosophizing altogether,
as is the case with some of the biblical theologians. For these
thinkers all insist that faith is essentially a commitment of the

E

whole personality, and not a detached act of intellectual judgment. I think they are in this matter mainly right, but I think they under-estimate the rational factor.

It is important to notice that in insisting on the moral element in religious faith, we are concerned with the essentials and not the trappings. Such matters as the dating and the authorship of books of the New Testament must be studied with all the intellectual detachment which scholarship demands; the canons of historical enquiry must be applied quite impartially. There is no moral obligation to defend, say, the physical miracles recorded in the Bible. The tragedy is that by cluttering up the essential faith with non-essentials, Christians have often played into the hands of those all too willing to rationalize their bias as honest doubt.

Since writing this chapter, I have read Professor W. G. Maclagan's book *The Theological Frontier of Ethics*.[1] This is a most valuable contribution to the subject, and with much of it I am in full agreement. Since, however, there are a few passages which might be regarded as conflicting with my main contention in this chapter, I must offer some comments on them. It is a pity that in the nature of things one tends to give more prominence to one's minor disagreements with another's thesis than to one's general admiration for it.

On page 56 he writes: "On the one hand, it may be held that the claim of duty upon us, when it is considered, with a Kantian austerity, simply in itself, is a sort of absurdity: but that if we can suppose that the universe is somehow 'friendly' to moral obedience, then it makes sense, as it otherwise would not, to expect this obedience from us."

This might be considered a fair summary of my contention in this chapter. But he regards the purpose of "supporting" the moral claim, by placing it in a factual context, as a radical moral heresy. He insists that the claim of acknowledged duty, whatever its nature and origin, neither requires nor admits of justification by reference to what is other than itself.

[1] George Allen & Unwin, 1961.

He makes, however, one concession that he seems to regard as parenthetical, but which seems to me—writing perhaps more as a Christian minister than as a moral philosopher—to be central. In insisting on the importance of moral motives in a world in which we are strongly tempted to disobey our moral intuitions, I pointed out earlier in this chapter that certain metaphysical beliefs carry with them emotional overtones strengthening our power to resist temptation. Now Professor Maclagan admits, on page 57, that even an intellectual dissatisfaction with the concept of duty—an inability to make sense of it—could, as a matter of psychology, affect moral practice. That was my point. You cannot make sense of the notion of objective moral obligation if your metaphysical background is atheism, and, as a matter of psychology, this is bound to weaken the moral will of any person who has a deep desire to make sense of his life.

But, as philosopher, Professor Maclagan wants to abstract from moral psychology, and deal with the matter as one of pure ethical theory. But even here I must contest his statement that the claim of acknowledged duty neither requires nor admits of justification by reference to what is other than itself.

In my view one can concede this contention only if one can regard it as tautologous—if, that is, one can interpret it as a statement that our awareness of the categorical imperative by its very nature binds us not to try to question it even to the extent of trying to account for it, and that therefore we must not try to account for it. But are we aware of a categorical imperative of this *extreme* nature? A considerable body of modern philosophers have denied that we are intuitively aware of *any* degree of objective moral obligation, and even in the remote past there have been subjectivist theories of ethics. I agree with Professor Maclagan that there is an objective obligation on us to do the right. But I frankly confess that if I could not make sense of it by seeing how beautifully it fits into my metaphysical picture, I should have to go over to the subjectivists. The categorical imperative cannot breathe in a metaphysical vacuum. It is one thing to say that an intuition of "ought" stands *initially* on its own feet, is not an inference from belief in God, and is in no way involved with the notion of punishment or reward. This might be true, although I doubt it. But it is quite another thing to say that in the mind of a rational being who wants to see life as a coherent whole, loyalty to such an intuition can be expected to maintain itself if his awareness that he has this intuition remains for him a brute fact, metaphysically isolated. He cannot be expected to reverence an alleged "duty" if it is for him an intruder in an objectively non-moral universe.

In this connection we must remind ourselves that we do not enter the world equipped with the notion of moral obligation. We acquire it only after long moral training. Children have to be offered inducements. Disinterested morality is psychologically possible only to those who have passed through a stage of interested morality—a stage in which reactions have been induced, reflexes conditioned. By all means let the moral philosopher plead for a logically prior ethical motive which is absolutely "pure". But the Christian Church is confronted with a practical moral problem. It is futile to tell a juvenile delinquent, who defiantly asks you why shouldn't he act anti-socially if he can get away with it, that the obligation to do right is categorical. People need a moral dynamic—not good advice but good news.

On page 62 Professor Maclagan writes: "Nor will it do to suggest that while the moral demand is not to be supported by the hypothesis of a friendly universe it can be . . . made more intelligible by it. To make the demand more intelligible would surely be to tell us something either about its nature or about its 'credentials'. But talk about the character of the world-context in which the demand presents itself is plainly not the former. . . ."

I must disagree strongly here. He is saying that talk about the context in which the moral demand appears can throw no light on its nature, and he evidently thinks that this is self-evident. But it is not in the least self-evident to one trained in the post-Kantian idealist school which teaches that the nature of anything *is* revealed by its relations to its context. Is our view of the nature of man identical whether we "explain" him in the God-context or in the chance-and-ape context? Is our view of the nature of moral obligation the same whether we place it in a God-context or a chance context?

He goes on: "Of course it is true that the hypothesis of a friendly universe would be 'illuminating' in the sense that it would remove the supposed *situational* absurdity of the occurrence of unconditional obligation in a neutral or hostile world. But to say this is not only irrelevant: it is an irrelevant tautology."

Now Maclagan seems to be distinguishing two sorts of absurdity. There is the situational absurdity which is merely an absurd situation—an anomaly or incongruity. Such situations are often portrayed in novels and on the stage. They do not contain any logical absurdity—they are not self-contradictory; and therefore they really can be; they can happen. But there are logical absurdities, contradictions, and when we are confronted by these we say, "we are not seeing the thing rightly. It cannot *really* be that. There is an element of false appearance, of illusion, in it."

Now Maclagan seems to be arguing that the fact of the moral demand in a non-moral universe, creates at most a situational absurdity, although in the next paragraph he doubts whether there is even that. He thinks that *no* sort of absurdity is involved by the conjunction of the fact of the moral demand and the fact of a hostile universe.

Now here I disagree. Not only is there a situational absurdity —a fantastic situation which a demoniac playwright might delight to portray—a bad universe which somehow produces people with a sense of moral obligation, but there is an actual logical absurdity. I am not thinking of the scholastic or traditional logic. If we use the word "logic" in *that* sense, you get absurdity only when you get formal contradiction; e.g. "All

S is P; some S is not P", and admittedly the case before us does not involve such contradiction. But I am thinking of neo-Hegelian logicians like Bradley and Bosanquet, whose treatment of logic is so much more empirical and psychological. These writers paid far more attention to the way in which rational people actually do reason. Now it cannot be denied that in ordinary everyday thinking, quite apart from our thinking about God and ethics, certain beliefs "go with" other beliefs. A certain degree of coherence is demanded by our rational natures. People who hold belief A will quite reasonably hold C and E, whereas people who hold B will reasonably dismiss C and E and hold D and F. Now consider the belief that I ought to be honest, interpreted in the sense that honesty is regarded as a human duty which would remain a human duty if every human being denied it. He who holds this belief holds that the statement "One ought to be honest" is as independent of human emotions and attitudes as is the statement that two threes make six. Now it surely must be admitted that such a belief coheres much more with the belief that there is some sort of Objective Moral Mind than with the belief that reality is atoms or sensa or anything impersonal, and that human beings "evolved by chance". There *is* a logical absurdity in the conjunction of a belief in objective moral obligation with a belief in scientific materialism.

But I should be sorry to give the impression that I am in radical disagreement with Professor Maclagan's main thesis. Our divergence is concerned with expression and with emphasis rather than with substance. This is clear from pages 63 and 64 of his book. He says, in effect, that if a man accepts unreservedly the fact of moral obligation without trying to make sense of it, he may well come to feel not only that the pessimistic hypothesis about the universe *ought* not to be true but that it *cannot* be true; he "feels it in his bones". This is, fundamentally, my thesis, except that I do not think it accurate to speak of "feeling" that a proposition is true. Decision that a proposition is true, even if an intensity emotional decision, must be fundamentally a decision of one's reason. Once one has come to cognize the connection between the notion of morals and the notion of a friendly universe, then, for ever after, doubt about the friendliness of the universe must involve doubt about morals, and this doubt is an affair not merely of feelings but of cognition.

One can make a strong case for regarding philosophy as a search for more and more adequate definitions, starting, of course, from initial provisional definitions. An instance of this, I suggest, is the present discussion. We must not bring God in at the start; we begin describing our moral sense in the barest way. But we end with a far richer conception of what the moral sense implies *and what, therefore, it really is*.

One can be so keen a moralist that, without being an atheist or emotionally hostile to the Christian faith, one will want to keep open a line of retreat to the last ditch of bare morality in case theism cannot ultimately be sustained. I think this bad tactics—in the interests of morality itself. As in war, caution can defeat itself; the commander who risked all on an advance has sometimes proved right. In the long run truth will prove sound tactics. I am prepared to risk all on the thesis "No God, no categorical imperative".

CHAPTER 4

Human Survival of Bodily Death

IN THE last chapter we arrived at a vital conclusion; it can be summarized as follows: There can be no more effective way of diminishing respect for the moral law than by propagating the belief that whatever forces or gods produced us are indifferent to morality. I wish to link that conclusion to the present chapter by a second proposition. There can be no more effective way of propagating the belief that whatever forces or gods produced us are indifferent to morality than by propagating the belief that all human beings, good and bad alike, are exterminated by the death of their bodies.

The question which I propose to discuss in this chapter is this: Does the innate teleology of the human mind demand the belief that human beings can survive death?

First, I must indicate what I understand by the phrase "The innate teleology of the human mind". In the physical sciences, such as mechanics, physics and chemistry, we are content to explain events by pointing to earlier causes, and these causes are not regarded as consciously aiming at the production of their effects. We think of the causes as blind or aimless. But when we speak of the innate teleology of the human mind we mean the innate tendency of human beings to demand explanations not in terms of blind past causes, but of future ends. The little child who plagues us with his continual "Why?" usually means "What for?" Indeed, he often says so. When he gets older he asks, "What's the use? What end or purpose is served?" But this search for purpose does not go on in a vacuum. It is inbreathed by an equally innate desire for meaning and for beauty, and by that passion for justice which inspires even small children, when playing their games, to cry out, "It isn't fair!" And so we tend to ask not merely, "What's the use" but, "What's the *good*?" And we cannot set arbitrary limits to this enquiry. In the end it leads to the question, "What good purpose is served by the existence of the human race?"

I have now to discuss whether such innate teleology demands that human beings can survive death. There are, however, those who will say that this will be a waste of time. For even if the fundamental postulates of human thinking, when analysed and rendered coherent and consistent, involve *belief* that we can survive death, this, they would say, is no evidence that the belief is true. Human thinking is one thing; objective fact is another. To prove that we want, or even that we need, a thing is not to prove that we shall get it.

This objection, in its present context, is based on a false view of the relation between the human thinker and the Universe. It is based on that confusion between the language of physical science and the language of constructive philosophy which inspires the loose talk about Copernicus having removed man from the centre and put him, with his puny hopes and purposes, on the outskirts of a vast Universe which is indifferent to him. Copernicus did nothing of the sort, as I have shown in Chapter 2. Copernicus's work was entirely in the field of physical science. He merely discovered that our respective perceptual fields could be related by a much simpler and more powerful mathematical calculus if each scientist used a system of co-ordinates in which his sun-percept was chosen as the origin rather than his earth-percept. The question of where we put our origin is entirely one of convenience, and it is absurd to say that Copernicus "proved that the earth is not the centre of the Universe". The superiority of Copernican over Ptolemaic astronomy is merely in its efficiency as a human instrument for the task of co-ordinating our actions in our respective conceptual fields and reacting to our respective perceptual experiences. The most interesting and important thing about the work of Copernicus is its revelation of the greatness of Copernicus—the efficiency of human thinking at its best. If we *must* use such metaphors, we can, indeed, point to him as an example of the fact than man *is* the centre of the Universe. The basic realities are the observers; language about what is observed is open to a wide choice; it is largely a matter of convenience.

We now have in our hands the answer to the objection. Of course many human desires are unsatisfied! We can acquiesce in this; it helps to make moral sense of life; it fits the view that human life on earth is a moral training-ground. But we are here concerned with the permanent and widespread longing of men at their best. Our decision on this question of human survival after death must turn on our decision as to what man *is*—his place in the scheme of things. Now, nothing more reveals his essential nature than does the innate teleology of his thinking, his conviction that somehow life must make moral sense and that since it does not make moral sense if this life is all, there must be a hereafter. Man, with his hopes and his fundamental concepts or categories, does not stand *outside* reality; he is what he is, and hopes what he hopes, because reality is what it is. His thoughts and his hopes are data for philosophy, far more truly so and far more revealing than any of the data studied by the physical scientist.

When we were children, we used to play a party game in which someone had to find a hidden article. Those in the know used to call out, when he got near it, "You're getting warm!" The human mind, in its quest for the truth about the things that matter most, is getting warmest when it meditates on its own deepest hopes and needs. The self-consciousness which divides man from the brutes contains the key to reality.

I have said enough to justify my insistence that in our study of the question of human survival of death the fact that our thinking is essentially teleological cannot be ruled out as irrelevant. We can, therefore, discuss the moral argument for survival without feeling that we are wasting our time.

One thing may be said in passing. If the moral argument leads us to postulate survival—if, that is, our belief in survival after death is based upon our belief in cosmic moral purpose and therefore in God—we can dismiss as unimportant the question, "How do the dead rise and with what body do they come?" (I Cor. XV.) We certainly do not have to believe in "disembodied spirits"; we can leave the *modus operandi* to God. He who created us can re-create us, with the memories which constitute identity. There is no difficulty in believing that God can re-create a psychosomatic unity. This is by no means a crude belief in the resurrection of the fleshly body. St. Paul would certainly have agreed.

And so we come to our question. Does the innate teleology of the human mind demand survival? We could, of course, try to settle the matter by taking a Gallup Poll. But the result would not be interesting or important. A person's deepest needs do not necessarily lie open to his own gaze, and no psychologist would take at their face value the answers to questionnaires about them. A more fruitful method will be to ask whether a denial of survival of death introduces an element of disharmony and frustration into human teleology. I believe the answer to be "Yes", and this in spite of the fact that the majority of people may not diagnose their case thus. I believe that if we cannot survive death, we have to face the fact that the major human purposes are doomed to defeat because they conflict with the nature of things. That would be a tragic state of affairs, but that is not my point at the moment. My point is that if we admit an essential conflict between human nature and the nature of things, we are faced with an acute *intellectual* problem. For man is organic to nature; he is an *expression* of the nature of things; he is part of the scheme of things.

I shall now show that if we will honestly face the facts and rigorously draw out their implications, we shall see that the denial of a hereafter leaves us with a view of life as both futile and evil. The majority of people do not see this because they are not given to facing unpleasant facts and rigorously drawing out implications. Their innate teleology has been stifled by the world, the flesh and the devil.

The first point I wish to make is that the denial of immortality frustrates moral purpose. Take the case of an intelligent juvenile delinquent who regards society's past efforts morally to condition his reflexes as having been merely an attempt on society's part to get him to subordinate his interests to society's interests. Now if that is all that morality is, he will naturally ask why *should* he thus subordinate his interests, and if that is all that morality is I do not know the answer. It is no use telling him that for our earthly lives morality is enlightened self-interest and that virtue is its own reward. For this is plainly false. The fact is, it is no use offering him good advice; what he needs is good news. He has got to believe that in the long run it will be better for him if he is good.

"But surely," someone will say, "you are not going to offer heaven as a bribe to virtue?" You appear to be shocked; but it is, surely, far more shocking to think of the scheme of things as so utterly indifferent to moral distinctions as to exterminate good and bad alike. The postulate that we can survive death is needed, not indeed to be the conscious motive of every moral choice, but in order to vindicate the moral reasonableness of the scheme of things. I do not think we can so lightly wave aside the notion of reward in heaven as some superior people wish to. We have to make an important distinction in this matter of the reward of the good life. Let me give an illustration.

On the one hand, I may say to a schoolboy, "If you work hard so as to pass your music examination, I will take you to the circus." This is a bribe. But on the other hand, I may say, "Work hard at your music, and you will then get so keen that the reward you will value most will be a scholarship to the Royal College of Music." This is *not* a bribe. Indeed, no one who had not been thrilled by music would want to enter the Royal College. Now, according to the Christian conception, going to heaven is much more like going to a Royal College than going to a circus. The reward of leading a good life is first to want, and second to be able, to go on to lead a better one. To offer this is not to offer a bribe. Indeed, without it moral exhortations do not make sense.

Another fundamental purpose of human life at its best is the quest for deeper and richer experience. Theists interpret this as the quest for God. We should not, of course, be seeking such experience unless in small measure we had already discovered it. It takes many forms, but in all there is a curious blending of joy and longing. In C. S. Lewis's book, *Surprised by Joy*, he tells of early experiences in which he found himself desiring "with almost sickening intensity something never to be described", and then found himself falling out of the desire and wishing himself back in it. For this unsatisfied desire is itself more desirable than any other satisfaction. Since the desire is unsatisfied, it has kinship with sorrow, and yet no one who has tasted it would exchange it for all the pleasures of the world. When I read that passage, I knew what Professor Lewis meant.

Now such experiences are crucial for our interpretation of human life. Are they the momentary opening of the prison door, yielding a passing glimpse of a glorious yet real world outside, into which physical death can release us? Or has no door been opened; are the experiences merely paintings on the inside of the prison wall—done by myself, in a moment of fantasy? The innate teleology of millions of souls has conceived of the first—the glorious—interpretation. If they are deluded, if death is the end, then we must accept the second interpretation. In that case the scheme of things is utterly cynical; it has prompted men to conceive of life as gloriously significant, while it mocks them and frustrates the hopes it has itself implanted. If men come to believe *that*, they will surely tend to regard the study of religion as merely the study of illusion—a matter for the mental pathologist; or they may be content to say that the religious man is a super-ape who has come over all sentimental.

Another conviction essential to a high moral purpose is that of the importance of the individual. Indeed, all morality turns on that. But the reflective mind must surely ask whether it is reasonable to set a higher value upon the individual than is set by whatever gods or forces rule the world. If we deny individual survival, the fact must be faced that the Universe kills off good men and bad men alike, as it kills off flies; it cares nothing for moral values, and contemptuously rejects the individual's idea that he matters. We can, of course, shake our fists at reality and say, "I *will* value men even if you don't!" Or we can say, "Let us treat our fellows *as though* they were important." But is defiance or pretence a sound basis for morality? Are men likely, if that view of life becomes universal, to have the heart to project into reality a morality which has no roots in reality?

"But," you may say, "it is not a question of pretending or defying. We can freely create worthy ends to govern our conduct and give life purpose. Can we not make life significant by dedicating it to the service of others—even of generations yet unborn?" Well, you can try. But your rational faculties will have to wear blinkers. Otherwise you will find yourself saying to yourself, "Here am I, of no value in the scheme of things, trying to give myself a value as a means to some end greater than myself. But what is this greater end? Merely others like me—of no more value than I am. It doesn't make sense."

One conclusion is clear. If man is but a super-ape, necessarily exterminated when his body dies, then the totalitarian ruler who treats individuals as pawns in his game is at least being realistic.

We seem to be approaching a very fundamental question. Readers of *1066 and All That* will remember that the authors had a way of commenting, "That was a Good Thing". Now human evolution is a process in which blind obedience to instinct and impulse tends to be replaced by a rational *criticism* of instincts and impulses—a process which had been applied, for example, to taboos about sex. It is inevitable, particularly as leisure increases, that the instinct for self-preservation, in individuals and in the race, will come up for scrutiny. Men

will seriously ask, "Is the human race a Good Thing?" We have
not quite got to that stage yet; indeed, I can think of one well-
known philosopher who has told us that human life is so horrible that there cannot possibly be a good God, and yet who
is getting worried lest this horrible thing should be exterminated by nuclear warfare. There seems an element of inconsis-
tency. But although the logical mills grind slowly, they do
grind, and sooner or later men will face the fact that if the
scheme of things is as futile and non-moral as a denial of immortality implies, then, if we still try to cling precariously to the
notion of duty, our duty may well be not to *prolong*, but to
exterminate, the race. What moral right have we to secure a
happy earthly existence for some by perpetuating unhappiness
for others? What guarantee is there that folly and evil will not
continue to dominate the human scene indefinitely?

I have known of agnostics who have urged that the real task
before anyone acutely concerned over the struggle between
good and evil was somehow to induce a religious fervour while
accepting death as final. The answer is that the thing cannot be
done.

One of the acutest minds of the Victorian age, a Cambridge
philosopher who was honest enough to forgo academic prefer-
ment rather than subscribe to the Thirty-nine articles, pon-
dered deeply on the question of human survival of death. Professor Broad referred to this great man's conclusions in the
following words:[1]

> "It seemed to Sidgwick, and it seems to me, that unless
> some men survive the death of their bodies, the life of the
> individual and of the human race is
>
> 'a tale
> Told by an idiot, full of sound and fury,
> Signifying nothing'"

Dr. Broad adds that survival is a necessary condition if the
life of humanity is to be more than a second-rate farce.

[1] *Religion, Philosophy and Psychical Research*, p. 114.

But I must not end this chapter on this gloomy note. My argument is really what we used to call, in the days when we did Euclid, a *reductio ad absurdum*. We proved a proposition by denying it and then rigorously drawing out the implications of our denial. When we found these impossible, we were forced to admit the truth of our original proposition. I have tried to show what is logically involved in the denial of the faith that we can survive death. If we cannot accept the implications of the denial, we cannot persist in the denial itself.

CHAPTER 5

The Christian Concept of Human Individuality

WHEN ONE is discussing the question of human survival of death, it is not uncommon to find thoughtful people saying something to this effect: "I feel difficulty with all the usual pictures of life in the world to come—the conventional harp-playing heaven and the idea of endless rest or endless religious services. I feel convinced that death cannot be the end, and yet beyond this negative statement I feel I cannot go."

The object of this chapter is to consider the *minimum* that is involved in saying that physical death is not the end—that in some sense we survive death. I shall not waste time considering mere word-play, for example, "to live in hearts we leave behind is not to die", or "we live on in our children". I shall be asking what at least must be conceded if in any real sense we are to envisage survival of human personality.

An example of the need for the closer analysis of the idea of survival which I offer in this chapter is provided by the short work entitled *A Grief Observed* by N. W. Clerk,[1] which has come into my hands as I write. In the early part of this, the author emphasizes our complete inability to conceive life beyond death. "Kind people have said to me 'She is with God'. In one sense that is most certain. She is, like God, incomprehensible and unimaginable". And he is contemptuous about "family reunions 'on the further shore' pictured in entirely earthly terms". And yet, as we read on, we find that he is far from questioning the essential Christian doctrine of eternal life. He

[1] Faber and Faber, 1961.

F

points to the apparent contradiction between our ideas of the mystical union on the one hand and the resurrection of the body on the other, and yet he firmly believes that Heaven will solve our problems, not by showing us subtle reconciliations between our notions but by knocking the notions from under our feet; "we shall see that there never was any problem". Now it seems to me that the kind of language he is using towards the end of the book—language which presupposes that *in some sense* human individuals live on—is justifiable only if we agree to attach a certain minimum meaning to the notion of individual survival. In one sense the departed are no more "incomprehensible and unimaginable" than they were when they lived with us on earth.

Let us imagine three men discussing this subject. The first says to me "You will survive the death of your body." This I find intelligible, in a way which I shall show. The second says "When your body dies, that is the end of you." This again has the merit of intelligibility. But the third says "You are immortal, but by this I mean that the Albert Memorial will be unaffected by the death of your body." I naturally feel mystified, and may even be provoked into asking him to talk sense.

"But," you will say, "does anyone ever say anything like this about death?" The answer is that there are people who tell me that I am immortal and then hasten to add that the *I* which is immortal is not what I call "I", but some other entity which, they assure me, is my real self. And when they try to explain this real self, it seems to me that even if it existed it could as little be identified with me as can the Albert Memorial.

This kind of loose thinking is often found in expositions of Eastern thought for Western readers. We are often told that the East has had deeper spiritual experience than the West. If this is true (which I doubt) it must be offset by the lesser critical capacity of the East—its weakness in the matter of analysing experience and integrating it into a coherent philosophy. It would be absurd, of course, to set experience and reason in antithesis; experience supplies the data, but reason must operate on the data before they can yield a credible whole to a critical mind. The mystic, as such, is far too easily satisfied with metaphor and myth; logical analysis is not his strong point. We must listen to him with respect, for he may have experienced more than we have. But we have every right to be critical if he evades difficulties by using metaphors, or if his language is inconsistent with itself or with the language of other mystics.

Now the question immediately before us is this. What constitutes the identity of individual personality over a period of time? The answer is that human individuality is characterized by an exclusive *memory* of a chronological series of experiences, the whole being dominated by implicit or explicit *purposes*. The memory, I repeat, is exclusive. I am I, in virtue of experiences and memories which are private to me. I am I, precisely because my present experiences, and my memories of past ones, exclude the private experiences and memories of other people. I am shut out from theirs and they are shut out from mine. And integrated with the memories are the purposes; we remember so that we can profit from the past in pursuing our purposes into the future. And because your memories and present experiences are different from mine, our purposes, although they may be similar are distinct and individual. You and I may both be striving to live for the glory of God; in that sense our purposes are one; but the environments which we seek to influence are distinct. A person, then, is a totality of *particular* memories and purposes; each person's memory is the memory of a single chronological series of events, and one's purposes, to a greater or lesser degree, form a unity. Ideally, as Plato held, the *good* life approximates to complete unity of purpose.

Now, one form of the Albert Memorial fallacy arises in the minds of people who have never faced this question of the nature of individual personal identity and who are, therefore, misled by loose thinking about the relation of a substance to its attributes. If, when I say that a lump of sugar is white, hard and cubical, I think I am talking about four entities—whiteness, hardness and cubicity, which are attributes, and a fourth entity, the substance which, as it were, underlies and supports the three attribute-entities, then I am being muddle-headed. To talk about the substance of the sugar is not to talk about a *fourth* entity; it is to talk about the *sole* entity there is—the entity which is the concrete unity of the three abstractions. The material substance does not exist apart from its attributes —its nature—and, conversely, the attributes cannot exist apart from the substance. Similarly with a human person. When we say that a person has sensations and memories and purposes, this does not mean that there exists a soul-substance which is a fourth entity, distinct from the three other kinds of entity— the sensations, the memories and the purposes. The words "sensation" and "memory" no more stand for entities than do the words "cubicity" or "whiteness". A person is a concrete unity of sensing, remembering and purposing.

The false notion that a substance is independent of its attributes leads quite logically to the equally false notion that the substance can be taken away and a new substance inserted, leaving the attributes unchanged. This has been the alleged explanation, to which Protestants object, of the real presence of our Lord in the consecrated elements. But, equally, this false notion leads to the idea that the substance could remain identical even though the attributes changed, so that we could say, "This piece of salt is really that lump of sugar which you saw a few moments ago; the attributes are quite different but the substance is the same." I have described these notions as *false*. But many modern philosophers would say that they are not so much false as meaningless, for we cognize a substance only by cognizing its attributes, and the assertions can, therefore, be neither verified nor falsified. But does anyone, in fact, say anything like this? Yes! The notion of reincarnation, or at any rate in its popular form, amounts to precisely this. A person is alleged to be the same person as one who lived long ago with different particular experiences, memories, and purposes. This is absurd, but I shall have to discuss it more fully. But first let me dwell for a moment on the vital connection between memory and personal identity and permanence.

Let us consider the sentence, "I hope to be alive after next Christmas." What I mean is that I hope that after next Christmas there will exist, either on earth or in some other sphere of existence, a self-conscious being whose memories of a chronological series of events will include, and will be recognized by him as *his own*, that series of remembered events which I now call *my own*. We need not raise the question whether his memories will be literally the same as, or will be merely similar to, my present ones, for this question is purely verbal. It does not arise exclusively over the matter of survival of death; it arises over my survival until tomorrow on earth. Will my tomorrow's memories of last year be the same as, or only similar to, my today's memories of last year? I can use which term I like; the facts are unaffected.

Each day our memories are added to; the sum total of tomorrow's memories will include today's with some additions. If, therefore, in any intelligible sense I can expect to survive the death of my body, I can expect that when my earthly life is ended there will exist a person whose memories, recognized by him as his own, will include those which I shall possess—in the sense of being capable of recalling—at my last self-conscious moment on earth. Conversely, if such a person will exist in "the hereafter", then that person will, by definition, be myself.

I must here add a word on the subject of identity-during-change. I pointed out that a substance and its attributes are mutually involved—whether a lump of sugar or a person. But there is a vital difference between the two cases. This mutual involvement, in the case of a material object, makes the question of identity a matter of degree. A new overcoat does not remain quite identical when a button is lost and replaced by another. When all the buttons have been replaced, and a large portion of the cloth has been re-patched, one can hardly claim it to be "the same coat". The process could, of course, be continued

till none of the original coat remained. It would then have lost
its original identity completely.

But the case of the identity of a self-conscious individual is
quite otherwise. Great changes may take place and yet we can
claim *absolute* identity. My outlook on life as an old man is
vastly different from that of my childhood. It may even be that
causes which I enthusiastically supported as a young man I
now oppose. My character may have deteriorated or improved.
I may now be much more like what Jones was at forty than
what *I* was at forty. And yet I have remained I throughout the
manifold changes of my life and Jones has remained Jones. In
what sense am I absolutely the same person as the schoolboy
of sixty years ago and an absolutely different person from
Jones? Clearly in the sense that my memories of a chronological series of events, recognized as *mine*, include those of
that schoolboy and exclude Jones's memory-series. Self-conscious memory confers an element of absoluteness on individual
identity which does not characterize the purely relative identity of material objects such as overcoats.

The self-conscious and self-remembering entity which we
call the self is absolutely unique. Can we call it a *substance*?
The answer is that if we are to use the term "substance" intelli-
gently, it *alone* is a substance! The very notion of substance is
derived from it. It alone has the precision which attaches to the
word. We have seen, for example, how difficult it could be to
decide whether an overcoat could be said to continue to be the
same substance or not. Again, is a chair one substance, one
"thing"? A carpenter, working by hand, who spends the morning carving the leg of a chair before fitting it to the seat, regards
the leg, while he is shaping it, as one thing. A row of chairs
nailed together, as is sometimes seen in public halls, is one
thing while it is being moved. The simple truth is that when
we think of any so-called material object as one thing or one
substance, we are projecting into it, for our convenience at
the moment, the notion of substance which we have acquired
from our experience of ourselves as individuals. Any selection

from my perceptual field I can treat as one thing, one substance, if for the moment it suits my purpose to do so.

All the difficulties over seeing how an entity can remain identical while it changes arise from our failing to notice the central truth about substance which I have just stated. Ancient philosophers saw that in a sense it seems contradictory to say that a thing remains the same and yet changes, but that nevertheless *it* could not be said to change unless it remains the same. The difficulty is quite unresolvable so long as we imagine that the notion of substance is derived from our contemplation of material objects. If we try to derive it thus we almost inevitably tend, as we have seen, to think of the substance as an entity separate from the attribute-entities, this mythical substance enduring while the attributes change. The truth, however, is that the root of the notion of permanence underlying change, of unity amid diversity, is the notion of the self. It unifies diversity by thinking of many things together; it remains identical by retaining the same memory-chain while constantly adding to it.

We are now in a position to see that it is absurd to say that *I* shall survive death unless you mean that the surviving entity of which you speak will remember, as *his own* experiences, the memories which will be mine up to the moment when old age or illness impairs my memory, or physical death detaches it, as it were, from my fleshly body. If you deny such survival of memory, you are in effect agreeing with the materialist who tells me that when my body dies *I* am exterminated. Moreover, the memory which guarantees identity must include full self-consciousness. To say that I shall exist but that I shall not be conscious of myself as an individual is as contradictory as it would be to say that a triangle will continue to exist but will have no corners. If it has no corners it will not be a triangle. If the alleged "I" has no memories which, as a self-conscious being, it claims as its own, it will not be "I" at all.

Dr. Leslie Weatherhead, in his lecture *The Case for Reincarnation*, tries to deal with this point. He asks, "What is more likely than that the formation of a new body means for most people the obliteration of the memories of an earlier life? Further, we cannot remember much of our own early years. Yet any psychologist would stress their importance. . . . We don't need to remember them to be influenced by them!"

Now it is true that there are many particular events in my past life which I have forgotten, but this is only because they are not specially interesting, or are the sort of things I do every day, like putting on my collar. (I have only a sort of *merged* memory of these last.) But it is quite possible—indeed, there is empirical support for the notion—that in certain circumstances, under hypnosis, for example, long-forgotten memories can be recalled. As we have seen in Chapter 2, our naïve picture or model of the so-called body-mind relation as the relation of candle to flame, the latter being entirely dependent on the former, is open to the gravest objection, as is also the picture of the brain as a sort of box with memories as things inside it. The relation of mental fact to physiological fact is very complex; it is certainly not a simple one-way dependence of mind on body. Brain injury can impair memory so long as the mind has a fleshly body, but against this must be set the vast evidence provided by psychical research that minds can inter-act without bodily functioning. The attempt to account for telepathy by "waves" is childish. There is no empirical evidence of waves; they certainly do not obey the inverse square law; and what sort of wave is it which, in cases of pre-cognition, arrives before it starts?

So Dr. Weatherhead's remarks about the obliteration of memories must not be taken as asserting obvious truth. And when he says that we do not need to remember events in order to be influenced by them he is saying something true but irrelevant, for the point at issue is not influence but identity. To be influenced by a life lived in the past is not to be identical with it.

It is not surprising that Dr. Weatherhead does not maintain this position consistently. In dealing with the natural human

desire (encouraged by our Lord's words to the penitent thief)
to meet again in heaven those we have loved on earth, he says
that our Lord's words "have taken away all fear of not meeting
my loved ones again". He seems to want to have it both ways.
When we ask how can we be identical with beings of whose
identity we have no memory, he says that memory is not
essential to identity. But he wants to retain the belief that we
shall meet our loved ones in the hereafter. But if we do not
remember *our* earthly lives, *a fortiori* we shall not remember
theirs. How then can we recognize them when we meet them?

The simple truth is that the Christian doctrine of man and
of heaven cannot be fitted into the reincarnation scheme at all.

But it may be asked, "are there not things which, in a future
life, we would much rather *not* remember—some painful experiences and, particularly, some of our sins?" That may well
be, but let us remind ourselves that there is a pathological side
to the desire to forget. Repression can lead to neurosis; even in
this life it is healthier to face our past, not evade it. Moreover,
to lose the *power* of recalling some part of our past is a depri-
vation, a depletion of personality. The Christian conception is
that the past is not forgotten but redeemed; if forgotten, how
could there be gratitude for forgiveness? Redemption is com-
pletion, not mutilation. How could it be the dying thief *himself* that went to paradise if all that was remembered there was
the last few minutes on the cross? If we are redeemed we no
longer seek to repress unhappy memories, for we see them in
a new context. Surely the greater perfection that will be ours
in the hereafter will include the power of recalling much *more*
than we can remember now—details which appeared pointless
but were really significant.

If there has been a purpose in, a meaning to, my earthly
discipline, if apparently meaningless accidents and incidents
have in God's providence been playing their part in my life,
surely when I see through a glass not darkly, as now, but
face to face, I shall see the pattern of it all. At present I may
be tempted to see my life as a muddle in a world of chaos. If

it is really a motif in God's symphony, surely I shall hear it thus in heaven. This *may* well involve recalling what now appears trivial; it certainly will involve recalling sins which I would, at this earthly stage, rather forget.

Some writers have suggested that each of us is made up of several selves. Which self, they ask, do we want to survive? Now, to refer to myself as made up of several selves is a gross abuse of language. There is, indeed, a conflict of *desires*; but they are all *my* desires; the strife is within *me*. You get a conflict between selves only when Smith is opposed to Jones.

We have here to guard against the uncritical reification of nouns—the tendency to think there must be some kind of entity corresponding to every noun we find it convenient to use. Nouns are often merely linguistic devices. Some of the worst offenders in this respect are the psycho-analysts—the Freudians with their ids and super-egos and censors, and, of course, *the* Unconscious, and Jung with his contrast between the ego and the alleged timeless self which existed before one's birth. If you tell me that Jones's self is now replacing his ego as the directing principle of his psyche, what you really mean is that at one time Jones wanted certain things and now he wants different things. Jones is an ontological unity, not a menagerie. We *must* distinguish ontological unity—identity of *being*—from ethical unity; confusion is caused when we talk of inner moral conflict as if it was an opposition of entities. Even philosophers have used such language as, "I refuse to identify myself with the self of yesterday that did a mean action". The ordinary, everyday phrase, "I disapprove of what I did yesterday", is quite adequate and far more accurate. If I do not identify myself with the bad self, how can I possibly repent? I cannot repent of someone else's sins!

The truth of the essential unity of the personality—a unity transcending all conflicts *within* the personality—is closely related to the fact that we are embodied beings. The Christian who understands his creed will not merely *admit*, he will *emphasize*, the close relation between consciousness and *some* form of body, for he holds that even in the hereafter we shall be embodied. The unity of the personality corresponds to the normal unity of the brain-and-nerve system. Multiple personality is a pathological state; when it is cured, the conscious unity—the integration of memories—is restored.

We are now in a position to comment on a passage in Dr. Weatherhead's lecture *The Case for Reincarnation*. He argues that William Tomkins loses his identity a number of times in the course of his life. There is the boy who gets tanned for being late at school; there is the youth who wrote "wet verses" to a girl with blonde plaits. "Do you want to assert your identity with him?" Then there is the William Tomkins who got sacked for dishonesty, "Do you feel robbed if he passes out of your sense of identity?" Finally there is the Tomkins with rheumatic joints and peering sight, whose body is now a nuisance. Is it really important that the *whole* personality of Tomkins shall go on indefinitely?

The answer, most emphatically, is "Yes!", once we have come to attach a precise meaning to talk about a personality "going on". We do not mean that we want Tomkins to remain the kind of person who wrote wet verses or robbed the till or feels rheumatic pains. But unless a William Tomkins survives who says, "I wrote wet verses, *I* robbed the till, *I* used to feel rheumatic pains", we may as well hand the whole case to the materialist and accept his verdict that when you are dead you are done with. The William Tomkins who is redeemed, who has progressed, will *know* that he has been redeemed, and has progressed, and will remember what he has been redeemed from. Otherwise the original William Tomkins has not been redeemed at all.

Notice the extraordinary nature of Dr. Weatherhead's argument. There is a number of separate entities classed together under the umbrella "William Tomkins". Each dies off in turn, but each *influences* those who come after, but only in the sort of external way in which, for example, Pitt the Elder influenced Pitt the Younger. At the end there will be no self-conscious being who will remember the series of Tomkinses as himself, and, Dr. Weatherhead tells us, it is far better so. But, nevertheless, when all these have passed away and are forgotten, yet "our true identity will not be lost; the pure gold of the ego will be maintained and strengthened". He offers no explanation of this "true" identity. He merely uses a metaphor—some gold is to be maintained and strengthened! To resort to metaphor when we are in a metaphysical hole is to admit defeat.

No view of human survival of death will be credible to thoughtful people unless it provides some answer to the question why the higher life of the future has to be preceded by the earthly life. Such a view must necessarily exhibit the moral character formed in the earthly life as being closely relevant to, and fitted for, the conditions in the new life. There has sometimes been a tendency of Christian writers, in their reaction against crude pictures of the hereafter, to emphasize the vast *difference* between the next life and the earthly life. But this raises a difficulty. If the boy's lessons in the fourth form are to prepare him for the lessons of the fifth form, the fifth form instruction must be continuous with that of the fourth form. There is surely continuity, not a sudden break, between the highest earth experiences and our first experiences in heaven. The memory which is so vital to the power of learning by experience—of growing in grace—the power of looking before and after, the memory which is essential to rationality and which separates us from the animals and links us to God—this is surely vital to that continuity of moral purpose which we must postulate if we are to believe in survival at all.

But the line of thinking which I am criticizing has a long history and is involved with a number of fallacies. We must examine it more closely. Its root idea is that an individual consists of distinct parts, or lives at distinct levels. There is an emphasis on the distinctness of the parts or levels and a failure to show exactly how, in spite of such distinctness, the parts or the levels are nevertheless the parts or the levels of one and the same individual.

A classic instance of this fallacy is the Greek notion that the human being consists of a bit of spirituality containing timeless abstractions or universals on the one hand, and a bit of sensuousness consisting of particular events participating in the time-flux on the other. Certain Greek philosophers had an incurable bias against particulars and a veneration for abstractions. It was, at bottom, intellectual snobbery; only the best people's minds work easily in the field of abstractions! In accordance with this bias they said that only the part of man dealing in timeless abstractions is worthy of immortality; the alleged part concerned with particulars—including one's awareness of oneself as a particular individual with one's memory of a chronological series of particular events—will be exterminated at death because it is so worthless. This fantastic way of talking has bedevilled philosophy and religion for centuries; even Christian mysticism has not escaped its influence, as we shall see.

We must attack it at the root. The simple truth is that our alleged knowledge of "universals" is not knowledge of a realm distinct from a realm of particulars. My awareness of particulars and my awareness of universals or abstractions are mutually involved. It is only because I am aware of particular red objects that I am aware of their common quality of redness. And the redness exists only as an adjective of particular red objects; there is no such entity as redness; there are only red objects.

The Greeks, and *a fortiori* other far less gifted ancient thinkers, never realized sufficiently the danger of picture-thinking and myth. They never sufficiently distinguished metaphor from metaphysic. Hence their view of man as consisting of two parts, or living at two levels—a higher bit consisting of universals or timeless abstractions, and a lower bit consisting of particulars in time. The lower bit crumbles away at death and the upper bit goes on existing.

If the alleged universal "part" of Brown is distinct from his existence as a particular individual—and if the universal part

of Jones is similarly distinct from *his* particular existence, how
is the universal Brown to be distinguished from the universal
Jones? There is, of course, no way of doing so, and so the universal "part" of each becomes the common features of all, and
it is only this abstraction, common to both, which goes on
existing when our bodies die. And then the argument is given
a curious twist. To this abstraction substance is ascribed, in
accordance with the reification fallacy to which we have referred. And then, to make the thing plausible, metaphors have to
be dragged in, and this reified abstraction, with special regard
to its aspect of consciousness or awareness or thought, is talked
of as the "root" or "ground" or "source" or "substratum" of
the particular existents. It is then given a name—Brahman,
for example.

There is, of course, a close relation between this procedure
and Plato's Theory of Ideas. Plato abstracted from particulars
—chairs, for example—the idea of their common feature, chair-
dom, endowed it with substance and talked as though particular
chairs derived their existence from, or "participated in" or
imitated the self-existent universal Chair. Modern philosophy
has rightly rejected this kind of talk; it is an outstanding
example of spurious metaphysics; it can neither be verified nor
falsified by experience, and it is not necessary to talk in this
way in order to account for any facts which could not otherwise be accounted for.

Now it is easy to see the connection between Plato's reasoning and the reasoning which I have been criticizing earlier.
Finite intelligences were regarded as deriving their being not
from the concrete existent God of the Hebrews, but from Mind-
in-General, or Universal Consciousness. Now it is one thing to
say, as the Hebrews did, and as I argued in the first section of
this book, that there must be some concrete existent Mind from
Whom we derive our being. It is quite another to abstract from
particular minds the notion of mind-in-general, abstract mind,
and then attach to it a label—"Brahman" or "The One" or even
"God". The height of absurdity is reached when this imagined

entity is called Reality and the particulars, from which it is merely an abstraction, are dismissed as "illusion".

Yet the essence of Hindu philosophy is "the identity of the individual soul, the Real Self, with Brahman the collective, universal consciousness".[2]

One very obvious difficulty with this line of reasoning is that an abstraction is poorer, not richer, than the particulars from which we derive it. How can the existence—or, if you fancy the term, the subsistence—of a being who is neither good nor bad but who has character-in-general, who is neither clever nor stupid but which has thought-capacity-in-general, account for the existence of the good Jones, the bad Brown, the clever Robinson or the stupid Smith? You really don't get over the difficulty by dubbing these gentlemen an illusion and saying that Brahman alone is Reality.

Sometimes we are invited to admire the wonderful insight of the mystic into the great truth that no predications can be made of The One. Actually no insight was needed if The One is a universal consciousness. It is the merest common sense that if you go on abstracting particular qualities from any alleged entity you end with the notion of being-in-general. The series table, wooden object, material object, ends in abstract being, just as does the series saint, human being, sentient being.

But we must criticize not only the absurdity of postulating a Real Self within each of us and identifying it with a Universal Consciousness; but also the tendency to wax lyrical over universals and pour contempt on particulars. What man ever fell in love with worthiness-to-be-loved or lovability in the abstract? He loves a particular woman. Love can exist only between particular concrete individuals. So with beauty. Even though we talk of beauty in the abstract, and spell it with a capital B, the fact remains that one's alleged perception of Beauty is always in the perception or imagination of particular beautiful things—this rose, this picture, this passage in this

[2] I have taken this phrase from Arthur Koestler's *The Lotus and the Robot*, p. 44. Hutchinson, 1960.

symphony. There is nothing vulgar or "lower" about particulars as such, and there would be nothing superior or "higher" about a realm of universals as such, even if it could be deemed to exist or "subsist".

This alleged separate and superior universal realm is also described as "timeless". According to the Graeco-Oriental way of talking, the inferiority of the realm of particulars is shown by the fact that particulars are subject to change, to temporal flow, whereas the universal realm is eternal, in the sense of *timeless*. We may well ask why the time-flux as such should be despised and timelessness as such venerated. It is due to a confusion of thought. Under the conditions of our earthly lives, time robs us of our youth, of the full vigour of our powers, and of our joys, and we tend to think of the flow of time with sadness or even bitterness. But it is confusion of thought to blame time *as such* for this. Indeed, we can glory in the time-flux when we reflect that time sometimes carries away our sorrows and pains, our immaturity and ignorance, and brings new joy. The nostalgic feeling which language about timelessness arouses in us is really a longing for *secure* joy and peace, its permanence *in* time, not its transcendence *of* time. We coin the word "timelessness" and use it glibly, but we cannot *imagine* timelessness. When we try to do so, we find ourselves imagining something persisting unchanged *in time*.

To discuss this adequately, we need to say something about mystical experience. We must distinguish between religious experience and mystical experience. The two may occur together, but they need not. Our Lord's words, "Blessed are the pure in heart, for they shall see God", certainly refer to religious experience, but it is certainly not true that the pure in heart necessarily have *mystical* experience. The capacity for having the kind of ecstatic experiences classed as mystical seems in many cases to have nothing to do with a moral character or religious faith. It seems to be an inherited capacity, sometimes with pathological accompaniments. It can be induced by fasting, or by learning a technique—deep breathing for example and self-hypnosis—or even by taking drugs. But there seems to be no reason for taking at their face value— taking as objective truth—the accounts of these experiences given by those who have had them.

For one thing, I cannot see why what is "seen" in an abnormal or trance state of mind should be taken to be "higher" or truer than what we come to believe by the use of our rational faculties. It is in virtue of our rationality, our self-conscious individuality, that we are superior to the animals and nearer to God. To fall into a dreamlike state, with our critical faculties suspended, is not necessarily to see truth. An ordinary dream, a day-dream, a mystical state, a hypnotic state—these are not identical, but they have this in common, that while they last, rational criticism is absent, and I fail to see why such absence should be deemed to endow the mystical state with superior insight into reality. After ordinary dreams one occasionally, on waking, remembers having seen the solution to some problem which has baffled mathematicians. One cannot, of course, remember the solution, and there is no reason to suppose that one really saw it at all; it was just a nice dream and there is nothing more to be said. One can, again, remember having been gloriously happy in an ordinary dream, but this affords no justification for referring to what one felt as "reality". If this is so with ordinary dreams, why should it be different in trance states? It is difficult to imagine a more perverse procedure than to label a trance vision Reality and contemptuously label the everyday world of joy and sorrow "illusion".

To regard religion as a technique for inducing states of bliss is far below the Christian ideal of the religious life. I am criticizing only trance-states, not religious experience. A type of experience which is not necessarily available to all those who believe in God, pray to Him, and strive to do His will, but which depends on some hereditary endowment or on a technique is, in my view, suspect. Genuine religious experience is surely the heightening, not the suspension, of our rational and moral consciousness.

G

With this parenthesis concerning mystical states, let us return to the alleged experience of timelessness. The notion of timelessness is quite capable of being reached, and was doubtless reached, by thinking at the normal level of discursive reasoning. It did not need mystical insight. As a matter of rational thought, we make a fundamental distinction between how the world *appears* to us and what is *really is*. If what we perceive or conceive presents us with contradictions or induces in us a sense of insoluble mystery we say that it is to that extent apparent and not real. Now the time-flux confronts us with mystery. We cannot believe that in seeing the Universe as an instantaneous present which is alone actual, for ever vanishing into a past of sheer non-existence, and in seeing a non-existent future for ever turning itself into an existent present—we cannot believe that in seeing the Universe like *that* we are seeing it "as it really is". Thus by a purely rational judgment, quite apart from any trance "insight", we affirm that Reality, or that the Divine awareness of Reality, goes beyond or transcends the time series as we know it. We must say "transcend" rather than "exclude" or "negate", for we cannot believe that the Divine awareness is ignorant of any experience of ours. God solves our time-problem not by negating our time experience but by including and supplementing it. "Timeless" is therefore quite the wrong description of Reality—of the Divine awareness. In small measure we can perhaps see in what direction our experience of time would have to expand to get nearer to the Divine. For even for *us* the past does not *entirely* vanish into nothingness. We can retain a vivid memory-image of past events; in that sense they are still present. And we can, in small measure, see the future in the sense of foreseeing what is going to happen. If I see a ball rolling fast along the table I can "see" in advance its falling to the floor and bouncing. If I see a batsman hit the ball out of the ground I can "see" in advance the umpire signal six and the scorer write it down. We can, then, think of the Divine Mind as retaining *all* the past and foreseeing *all* the future. But this does not mean that time-movement, even for Him is abolished.

The flow of time cannot just be dismissed as illusion. There must be something objective corresponding to the fact that for us all time flows "in the same direction". There is an objective distinction between past and future. Even the Special Theory of Relativity insists that if events are connected, for any observer, by a temporal vector, they must occur in that order for all observers.[3] Even the Divine awareness, then, must include time-awareness, although we cannot, of course, expect to know how He solves the "antinomies" which baffle us. (There really is no mystery in the fact that there are mysteries which we could not solve without being God!)

Although, therefore, we must think of God's awareness as transcending *our* time-awareness, we must not describe it as timeless. We cannot think of it as an ignorance—a sheer non-awareness—of anything of which *we* are aware. Even if, therefore, we had to believe that a human being can experience an expansion of consciousness towards the fullness of the Divine awareness, there is no reason to suppose that this would be an experience correctly described as "timeless". Our sense of time is not illusion, and if in trance-states one can really lose the sense of time (which I doubt) it is the trance state which is illusion, not our everyday consciousness.

Now, bearing in mind that the notion of timelessness is reached at the ordinary level of thought, let us notice that the content of trance-visions is certainly influenced by beliefs and ideas reached at this ordinary level or imbibed as part of one's early training. I doubt if any psychologist would deny this. But it is not only the content of the visions, it is also the language used in subsequently describing and interpreting them, that is so influenced. A person who has thus acquired the concept of timelessness and a nostalgic feeling about it, may, therefore, have trance experiences which he will describe as "timeless".

We are often invited to notice the similarities between the accounts of mystical experiences given by mystics of different religions, and it is suggested that this proves that in contrast

[3] See A. Kopff, *The Mathematical Theory of Relativity*, p. 42. Methuen.

with philosophers who fail to achieve agreement because they merely *reason*, the mystics reach agreement because they *see*. They apprehend by a simple process in which human interpretation is at a minimum. This line of argument exaggerates the extent of the agreement between mystics, and minimizes the extent to which their written accounts have influenced one another. Descriptions of mystical experience come down to us from the ancient world; this sort of language is part of the mental furniture of the minds of all educated people. Mystics have read or heard one another's language, and it provides a stock of phrases which spring to the mind when they try to utter the unutterable.

We need not, therefore, be impressed by the frequency of references to timelessness in mystical literature. For example, one writer goes so far as to say, "Duration has nothing to do with it. You cannot enjoy the Eternal for any length of time, long or short."[4] I cannot attach the least meaning to this statement, and I do not believe any finite being has ever had any experience of which such words are a perfectly accurate and adequate description. Negative statements can often be significant for they can imply some positive content, however vague; "not red" can suggest *some* other colour. But the above statement is a sheer negation which suggests nothing.

Let us notice that the mystic's trance occurs in the time series. An onlooker can say with confidence (assuming there was no shamming) that the mystic was entranced, or at any rate unconscious, for two minutes or for an hour. The onlooker could not, of course, say for what portion of this period the entranced person was actually having the experience, but it certainly looks as though the experience was not *in fact* timeless. Even if it occurred at a moment of time it was still an event in the time series.

We need not question the sincerity of the account of the experience given afterwards by the person who had it. We

[4] Geddes MacGregor, *Introduction to Religious Philosophy*. Macmillan, 1960.

need not, even, object to the use of the word "timeless" if it be admitted that it was being used as any imaginative writer or poet might have used it when writing literature and not psychological or philosophical analysis. If we are lying under a tree on a summer's day, with not a sound stirring, not a leaf moving, not even noticing our own breathing, we may afterwards say that time stood still. This is quite legitimate in descriptive writing. But it was not strictly accurate. There was a faint movement of attention; if it had ceased altogether the dreamy state would have become dreamless sleep. But can we seriously suggest that this dreamy state, in which our normal powers seem to be partly in abeyance, was more akin to the Divine Mind?

"But this," you will say, "is not the mystic's state of mind. He is not half asleep; he is acutely awake; he is in a state of increased awareness of reality." Very well! But this means that a finite being, over a period of time, long or short, was noticing something that interested and excited him. He remembers it and tries to find words to tell us about it later. He was not noticing the movements of his own attention; he was not *noticing* anything changing at all; it was not change but changelessness which was in the focus of his attention; he was attending to the changeless features of what he saw. This is all that it is necessary to admit in order to give a sufficient reason for his use of the word "timeless". He was not *attending* to change; but change there was.

But here I ought to refer to a passage of scripture which has been taken to justify the statement that life in the world to come will be timeless. Incidentally, this strengthens my contention that there is no need to regard the notion of timelessness as having been arrived at by direct mystical experience. I argued that it was arrived at by metaphysical thought at the ordinary conscious level. I must now point out that it was strengthened by a mistranslation of a passage in the Bible.

In verse 6 of chapter 10 of the Book of the Revelation, we read that an angel lifted up his hand to heaven and swore a most solemn oath that "there should be time no longer". It is very surprising to find this statement in the Bible, for two reasons. First, the notion of timelessness is contrary to the general trend of Hebrew thought. For the Hebrews time was real, and God was working time. The Hebrews believed in history —believed that God Himself was at work in time—that it was real in His sight as well as in ours. They put their millenium— their good time coming—in the *future*. So the statement, "There shall be time no longer", creates a real difficulty. Secondly, the statement does not fit the context. The chapter does not contain a metaphysical discussion. It is drama. Six angels have sounded their trumpets, and all sorts of exciting things have happened. The angel who swore the solemn oath follows up his alleged statement that time shall cease by saying that when the seventh angel sounds his trumpet, "then is finished the mystery of God". The context clearly demands, not the propagation of an abstruse metaphysical doctrine, but the statement that the end of waiting for the solution of the mystery is at hand. Even, then, if we had to translate the Greek by, "Time shall be no longer", we should have ample justification for taking it as merely a vivid way of saying that the present Age is coming to an end. But actually the translation is incorrect. "Chronos" here means not *time* but *delay*. The correct translation is, "There shall be no further delay".[5]

That the mistranslation has, however, caused the widespread notion that "eternity" is timeless is seen from Christian hymnaries. For example, a hymn by Wesley contains the couplet.

> "Thy love each believer shall gladly adore
> For ever and ever, when time is no more."

Doubtless Tennyson's "from out our bourne of time and place", was influenced by this same notion that timelessness is "scriptural". Notice, too, the contradiction contained in any language which puts timelessness before or after time—the

[5] See the Revised version margin. Also the translations of Weymouth, Moffat, Phillips, the American Revised Standard Version and the New English Bible.

idea of things happening before time began or after time is finished. Language about timelessness usually acquires a spurious appearance of being meaningful by covertly introducing time-concepts.

Some readers of the preceding exposition may have wondered whether I have been banging closed doors. Are the views I have been criticizing widely held, or held by people whose views need be taken seriously? I now propose to refer to certain published writings the reading of which has prompted me to write as I have done.

In the late Dr. Inge's *The Philosophy of Plotinus* (vol. II, p. 96) he tells us that Plotinus distinguished between "the lower soul-life, the surface consciousness and surface experience which make up the content of our sojourn here as known to ourselves", and a higher life in "the true home of the soul", a supra-temporal world, from which we are "banished" during our lower soul-life.

Note here the free use of metaphors. We know what it is, in our earthly life, to live in a home, and, on the contrary, to be banished to a strange land. At a first glance we might think that Plotinus is here merely picturing this earthly life as a banishment, and that the person accounted worthy of surviving bodily death is pictured as finding, on arriving in heaven, that it is the true home he has been subconsciously seeking. This would be a lovely idea, but an examination of the text does not bear out this interpretation. The "lower" soul-life is described as a "surface" consciousness; the inference is that there is a "deeper" consciousness. Then we have an alternative description of the surface-consciousness. It is our life "as known to ourselves". The surface consciousness is thus our ordinary everyday consciousness. The rest of Inge's exposition is an example of what I earlier called the Albert Memorial fallacy. The alleged "deeper consciousness" is referred to as our "real self", and there is nothing to distinguish this real self from the real selves of other people, and therefore from a Universal Consciousness. The true home of the soul, he tells us, is a "supra-temporal world", in contrast to the temporal flux in which our "surface" or "lower" soul-life is lived.

We find here that sheer dualism which we noticed in our earlier analysis. The surface consciousness and the deeper consciousness have no apparent connection. The surface consciousness is my ordinary everyday awareness of myself as an individual born at such-and-such a place and with such-and-such a history of particular experiences, a time-flux of sensations, percepts, desires, emotions, joys and sorrows. This, he tells us, is myself "as known to myself", and by implication the "deeper consciousness" is *not* known to myself.

The metaphor of banishment is thus a sheer abuse of language. There is no question of one and the same person being first banished and then at home. The banished person is quite different from whatever sort of entity is conceived to be "at home". What I call "I" dies, and the only immortality which Dean Inge offered us was the immortality of Something Else. He did not conceal his contempt for those who wished to prolong the surface-consciousness—the "self as known to myself". The looseness of his thought is apparent from the alternative language which he apparently regarded as equivalent. Those who have no wish to prolong the surface consciousness are described as having no wish "to prolong the conditions of their probation after the probation itself is ended". No one could quarrel with this. No spiritually minded person would wish to live in a "heaven" in which we continued to be frustrated by the tedious and trivial materialism of our earthly life. But Inge's language fails completely to establish the essential point that it is one and the same individual who experienced the probation, remembers that *he* has experienced it, and rejoices in the new freedom, finding it all the more glorious by contrast.

The reader may feel that I have read more into this passage than Inge intended. Let him therefore consider a further exposition of Inge's philosophy in *Outspoken Essays*. He tells us that "the interest of consciousness lies in the ideal values of which it is the bearer, not in its mere existence as a more refined kind of fact". If words mean anything, this means that we are being frivolous when we are interested in Nelson the man; it is the Courage of which his particular individual existence was an expression which alone matters, or "has value". Do we really believe this? Surely it is the particular Nelson, with his mixture of weakness and greatness, which both interests us and "has value". That is certainly the Christian view. The Shepherd left the ninety-and-nine and went out to seek a particular lost sheep, not a complex of eternal values. Inge's language betrays the clear contrast between the Graeco-Oriental bemusement with abstractions and contempt for the individual on the one hand, and the Christian insistence on the value of the individual on the other.

He then tells us that when Plotinus says that "nothing that really is can ever perish", and when Höffding says that "no value perishes out of the world", they are saying the same thing. "In so far as we can identify ourselves in thought and mind with the absolute values, we are sure of immortality". This clearly means that values alone are real; values alone are immortal. If I learn not to care about myself, to lose interest in myself, and become absorbed in the values, "identify myself with" the values, then the only thing I care about will live on; I need not dread my own extinction. And, therefore, I can speak of myself as immortal, for I have identified myself with what will never perish.

This is a good example of that mixture of myth and metaphor which used to pass for metaphysical profundity, and to which philosophical analysis is a legitimate reaction. It is also an example of that veneration for abstractions which we have noticed. There is not the slightest reason for holding that values as such exist or "subsist" on their own, apart from the particular conscious beings who have valuable qualities or who perform valuable actions. And there is no sense in taking literally the expression "identifying oneself with values". To be courageous is not, literally, to identify oneself with Courage. So that even if it made sense to talk of Courage as being an immortal Value it would not mean that to be courageous is to be immortal. The argument is merely a game with words.

A word should here be said about the use of metaphors in discussing matters of this kind. It is sometimes said that in discussing the things of the spirit we are bound to use metaphors drawn from the material world. This is not so. There are a number of purely psychological terms which are not metaphors— for example, the verbs to sense, to feel, to think, to remember, to infer, to plan, to purpose, to choose. It would be unnecessarily austere to say that metaphors should *never* be used; they often add vividness and force to the writing. But they should never be used to put over a thesis which could not be stated in non-metaphorical language—that is, to get away with a muddled notion or wriggle out of a difficulty. For example, after one has used a spatial metaphor to the effect that a consciousness is "merged" or "expanded" or "absorbed" or "raised" into a "larger" or "higher" one, one should ask whether what one wants to say can be stated with precision in psychological terms—whether, in fact, one can, without such metaphors, avoid the antithesis that an individual either continues his existence as a self-conscious individual remembering his past life, or is exterminated. The answer, is clearly "No!"

Towards the end of his discussion Dr. Inge himself mentions this matter of the use of metaphor. "We must remind ourselves", he says, "that we are using a spatial metaphor when we speak of a centre of consciousness." The point is that he has just written, "The question, however, is not whether in heaven the circumference of the soul's life is indefinitely enlarged, but whether the centre remains." And so, dropping the notion of a centre, he proceeds to say that the *individuality* is maintained in spite of the enlargement. He amplifies this as follows. "If every life in this world represents a unique purpose in the Divine mind, and if the end or meaning of soul-life, though striven for in time, has both its meaning and its source in eternity, this, the value and reality of the individual life, must remain as a distinct fact in the spiritual world."

But this is ambiguous. It could be taken to mean merely that in the Eternal Divine Consciousness there is an awareness of the part my life played in the drama, and it is not unfair, in the light of the context, to interpret it thus. But in no real sense is this my resurrection to new and higher life. To say that the values I have created or exemplified remain eternal objects for the Divine Consciousness is perfectly compatible with the assertion of my complete extermination.

This obsession with abstractions or universals, this horror of particulars which Inge derived from his enthusiasm for the Greeks, dominated his whole outlook. He tells us that "The man whom we love is not the changing psycho-physical organism; it is the Christ in him that we love, the perfect man who is struggling into existence in his life and growth". This is untrue. Love is an I-thou relation; a particular finite individual loves a particular finite individual. Inge was, of course, very near a great truth, but he spoiled it by over-stating it. If he had said that love for a human being is the glorious thing it is because man is made in God's image, and is not a super-ape evolved by chance and because a man is indwelt by God's spirit to the extent that he is good and lovable, then he would have been right. But the indwelling of God does not destroy my individuality and personality; it gives it value. It is through loving concrete individual men and women that we can love God. "If a man love not his brother whom he hath seen, how can he love God whom he hath not seen?" A means to an end need not be *merely* a means to an end; it can also be an end in itself. It is not sound Christian doctrine to regard love for people as *merely* a means to the end of loving God. The Christian view is based on the analogy of the family. Brothers and sisters love each other *and* their parents. Heaven is a Kingdom, a society, a communion of saints.

Dr. Inge's treatment of immortality in works published many years ago is reproduced in a recent work by Mr. Kenneth Walker, *So Great a Mystery*. Here again we have the division of a man into a "real" self and the other part. To call one part "real" clearly implies that the other part is unreal or illusory. We have already noticed the tendency of writers in the pre-analytical period to describe what they disapprove of as "unreal"; Mr. Walker clearly does disapprove of his everyday conscious personality. It is so worthless that he doesn't want it to survive. He sees no reason to believe that what he calls the "odd assortment of habits, traits, quirks and idiosyncrasies" which constitute his personality—the features by which his friends recognize him—should be accorded the privilege of continuing to live.

Now here again there is not the slightest *practical* difference between Mr. Walker's utterances on the subject and those of the crudest materialist. For it is only the alleged "real Self" that is to survive the death of the body. And what is this real Self? Well, I can take my choice. On the one hand he tells me that it is "of an entirely different nature to my personality and my body, and belongs to a different level of being". But if something is of an entirely different nature from myself, how can it be myself? I and my nature, my substance and my attributes, are not separable entities. On the other hand he tells me that my "real Self" is a universal something "Indivisible, but as if divided into beings".[6] But how can a universal something be *myself*, since my individuality is defined by what it excludes? Mr. Walker's "real Self" is the Albert Memorial.

In protest against the habit of labelling as unreal anything one wishes to disparage, including our everyday consciousness, I must insist that the everyday self whose moral character has been built up by moral decisions taken at the level of rational thought *is* the real self. One of the most characteristics heresies of the age is the habit of belittling conscious reasoning. It is the possession of self-conscious rationality that distinguishes men from animals. The person so dominated by unconscious motives that he ceases to exercise rational control is a pathological case. And to cure him is to help him to become conscious of his

[6] This a quotation, he tell us, from the *Bhagavad Gita*.

motives so that he can direct his actions rationally towards the realization of the ends characteristic of men as such. The expression "the real self" should be applied to the individual self formed by conscious decisions, whether right ones or wrong ones. There are on record, we are assured, cases of persons of saintly character who, in delirium, have used obscene language. The explanation, which seems quite feasible, is that their very horror of such language has made them repress it, so that when their self-conscious rationality temporarily ceased to control their speech organs, these repressed ideas took control. Surely we are not going to say that the language of delirium revealed their real selves!

Another instance of the language which I am criticizing is found in V. H. Mottram's *The Physical Basis of Personality*. He makes a sharp distinction on page 118 between the "personality" and the true self, the real "I". He refers to the saints who, in moments of mystical insight, seem to discern the existence of an "inner Self" beneath the personality, an inner self which "partakes of the nature of ultimate reality, by whatever name they call this reality—God, Allah, Yahveh, Brahman, the Absolute, Love or Wisdom."

I will not linger to criticize the expression "*ultimate* reality", although it needs a careful analysis which it never seems to get. But let us notice the wide range of names for it which Professor Mottram gives. He seems to suggest that all mystics perceive the same thing but call it by different names. This, as we have seen, is a very large assumption. Descriptions of mystical experiences are hopelessly involved with metaphysical assumptions of varying degrees of respectability. Notice also the spatial metaphors "inner" and "beneath", and the same tendency to describe what is seen in a trance-state as "real".

He then proceeds, in the style of Mr. Walker, to pour contempt on "this familiar thing which we call self, this assertive, greedy and sensual thing compact of egoism, selfish desires, odd moods and passions and of outstanding characteristics which we dub personality". We can guess what is coming! This self is "an imposture and delusion". Whose delusion? If it *is* a delusion how can it *have* a delusion?

It is amazing that scientists whose minds work so admirably in their own subjects should be so amateurish when they venture into metaphysics. What we dub "personality" is no more a delusion than is the fact of gravitational attraction. It exists, and you cannot prove its non-existence by calling it names! We get the usual appeal to metaphor. The alleged real "I" is the "core" of our being. And yet in the next sentence we are told that this core is *alien* from the everyday "I". We see here that contradiction which we noticed in Inge and Walker. They all want to have it both ways. Something is alien from, of a different nature from, on a different level from, my everyday personality. And yet they refer to it as *mine*, it is "the core of our being" (Mottram). It is, for all of them, *my* "real Self", and the word "my", indicates that the possessor is the everyday self. The everyday self possesses a real Self just as he possesses a real hat. And yet this real self is both the core of the possessor self and *alien to* the possessor self.

Professor Mottram then quotes, with no indication of disagreement, the view of Eastern philosophy that "there is deep within us a self, a soul, which is one with Ultimate Reality". So we have that same identification of the alleged "real self" with a universal self which I have criticized earlier.

It should here be noticed that any experience, however ecstatic and whatever the person himself may say about it later, is the experience of an individual person. It is not an "escape" out of individuality into something wider. It is all the more necessary to insist on this since this talk about "escape" is not uncommon in mystical literature. For example, Mr. Aldous Huxley, in *The Doors of Perception*, writes of "the urge to escape, the longing to transcend themselves if only for a few moments", as having always been "one of the principle appetites of the soul", and he claims to have effected such a temporary escape by taking the drug mescalin. But the vital point to notice is that Mr. Huxley returned to a normal state of consciousness, in which he remembered the experience—remembered it as *his*—and wrote an account of it. The experience of "escape" was, then, one of the units in the private and exclusive memory-chain constituting life of an individual. Of course, it is quite legitimate to speak of this as a temporary escape of an individual into a wider-than-normal *environment*. But it was not an escape out of individuality itself. It was an experience in which a person was not noticing his individual existence, but concentrating on something objective and exciting. But this often happens even in normal consciousness. A football enthusiast has his mind on the game; he may not give a thought to his own existence *while the game lasts*. He "escaped from himself" or from troubles, in a purely metaphorical sense. But to say that an individual has "escaped" into a wider consciousness and will *nevermore* think of his consciousness and his memories as *his*, is to say that he has been exterminated.

"But," someone might say, "may it not be that in heaven a person will be so taken up with contemplating God that he will lose consciousness of himself?"

Let us consider this carefully. When, in our everyday earthly life, we say that we are self-conscious, we do not mean that at every moment of the day each of us is thinking about himself. For long periods we can think objectively—can be absorbed on some task or on watching a game without giving a thought to oneself. But we do mean that we have the capacity for, as it were, swinging our attention on to ourselves, and possibly relating what we have been thinking about to the fact that it is we who have been thinking. It is this capacity which raises us above the brutes.

A sound philosophy will see in self-consciousness something that links us to God, not something to be despised. If Jones is to be conceived as eternally contemplating God in heaven and as having lost the capacity which he had on earth of being explicitly aware of what he is doing and of himself as doing it, then he will have sunk, not risen, in the scale of being.

One of the fallacies of Buddhism is the notion that there is something essentially proud, and therefore evil, in the thought "I exist". This notion would be correct if self-awareness necessarily involved selfishness. But it does not. On the contrary, the higher forms of virtue, including intelligent altruism, would be impossible were we incapable of self-examination.

But there is a further objection. If Jones's life in the world to come is pure objective contemplation of God, divorced from self-awareness and from memories of his earthly life, and if Brown's life in the world to come is exactly similar in this regard, how is Jones's life to be distinguished from Brown's? Both are impersonal contemplations of God; why do you call one of them Jones's and another Brown's. In what way is what you call the Jones's contemplation of God in any sense a continuation of the Jones earthly life?

The moral of all this is that we must not be bemused by metaphors about escaping from ourselves. A person can escape from himself only by ceasing to exist. If the life of the world to come could, *per impossibile*, be accurately described as a place where one had escaped from oneself and been lost in God, it could not be described as a place where finite beings loved God or had a beatific vision of God. To love, or to have a vision, one has to exist; to "escape from oneself" and be lost in God is to cease to exist.

It is often said that the distinguishing characteristic of Christian, as distinct from certain, although not all, of the non-Christian mystics, is that the Christian mystic denies that the individual loses his individuality on the death of his body. This is broadly true, but unfortunately even Christian mystics have a way of indulging in a riot of metaphor when describing their visions, and this can lead to misunderstandings. In Professor Zaehner's *Mysticism, Sacred and Profane,*[7] he explicitly contrasts theistic mysticism with pantheistic monism. He points out on page 172 that in monism there may be ecstasy and trance and deep peace, but there can be no love. He means, I take it, that even if one *could* intelligibly be said to have be-

[7] O.U.P., 1957.

come one with a larger whole, one could not be said to *love* it, for love, in the accepted usage, is essentially a relation between at least two minds. But in making this distinction between monistic and theistic mysticism Professor Zaehner refers to all mystics, Christian and pagan alike, as seeking for "loss of self" in God. One must assume that he is here using a metaphor, and means a loss of selfish *desires*. The Christian certainly does not seek a permanent loss of self-awareness. Selfish desires link us to the Devil; self-awareness links us to God.

Another instance of this ambiguity can be quoted from St. Teresa.[8] She is speaking of four levels of prayer. At the highest level she tells us that "The soul enjoys undoubting certitude; the faculties work without effort and without consciousness; the heart loves and does not know that it loves; the mind perceives and does not know that it perceives. If the butterfly pauses to say to itself how prettily it is flying, the shining wings fall off and it drops and dies. The life of the spirit is not our life, but the life of God within us."

This is so obviously sincere that one hesitates to criticize. But difficulties must be faced. Assuming that she was describing her actual experience, the simple fact is that she *remembered* the loving and perceiving and said to herself, in effect, "*I* loved and *I* perceived." She did not, therefore, *lose* self-consciousness. And the sin of the butterfly was not its awareness that it was flying but its pride in the flight. Moreover, to say that the life of the spirit is the life of God within us is sound Christian doctrine, but to say that the life of God within me is *not* my life is to treat the man who is "born again" as a split personality. It is to treat all that is *mine* as essentially evil or worthless and therefore mortal. The truly Christian view is that the sinner, just as he is, can be forgiven and redeemed, and that the life of God is within me is *my* life.

The nostalgic feeling aroused in us by language about escaping from ourselves is not difficult to account for. One gets tired

[8] Quoted in J. A. Froude's essay in *The Spanish Story of the Armada and other Essays*. Longmans, 1904.

H

of one's environment, one's prosaic and petty thoughts; one longs to escape into a larger and richer existence. But one wants *oneself* to have the new experience—not that someone else shall have it. This is not a desire to escape *from oneself*! But if one longs to escape from the problems which self-awareness brings by ceasing to be aware of oneself, this is pathological; it is unhealthy escapism.

Whilst on this subject of the alleged possibility of escaping from oneself, I will refer to a passage in W. T. Stace's essay "Broad's views on Religion" in *The Philosophy of C. D. Broad.*[9] He quotes from Koestler's *The Invisible Writing*, page 352, "Then I was floating on my back in a river of peace under bridges of silence. It came from nowhere and flowed everywhere. Then there was no river and there was no I. The I had ceased to exist. . . . The 'I' ceases to exist because it has by a kind of mental osmosis established communication with, and been dissolved in, the universal pool."

If this were merely a piece of imaginative writing we could let it go at that. But it is presumably offered—at least, that is how Stace interprets it—as serious philosophy. We are, therefore, entitled to analyse it. At once we see the contradiction to which I have already called attention. "The I had ceased to exist". But had it? Only if we can equally say that whenever I am not thinking about myself, when for example, I am doing mathematics, I cease to exist. When I remember my past life as a chronological succession of private experiences it is true that I do not claim that these experiences exhibit completely continuous self-consciousness; there are gaps during sleep, and there were periods, longer or shorter, in which I was thinking objectively and when, therefore, the fact of my own existence was not in the focus of attention. But this does not prevent my saying, in everyday language, that I have existed as an individual for, say, seventy years. Now, whatever experiences Koestler is describing when he talks about there being no I and about its having been dissolved in a universal

[9] *The Library of Living Philosophers*. Tudor Press, New York, 1959.

pool, the simple fact remains that they were his experiences, they are part of that memory-chain the possession of which constitutes individual identity. For if they were not, he would not be able to recall having them now. I would go farther. If he explicitly *noticed* that there was no I, he must have been thinking about himself, must have been aware of the I. If I say, "The last apple has gone from that tree", I may fairly be said to be thinking about an apple! If I can *notice* that I have been dissolved in a Universal Pool, it is clear that I have *not* been dissolved in a universal pool.

But the height of absurdity is reached when Stace goes on to say, "It is false that consciousness is necessarily associated with an 'I'. There is a universal consciousness to which even human beings can attain, and this universal consciousness in which all individual egos dissolve and cease to be distinguished from one another is the divine consciousness."

I have already protested against the habit of slipping into metaphors when in logical difficulties. Why does he say "dissolve and cease to be distinguished from one another?" Why not say that the individual egos are exterminated and leave it at that? How can *I* be intelligibly said to "attain" something if I am to be "dissolved" and become indistinguishable from anyone else?

Moreover, Stace says that there is a universal or divine consciousness which is not aware of individuals as such. But surely in describing this as *a* consciousness he shows that he regards it as *having* unity; but by denying that it is associated with an 'I' he is denying that it is *aware* of itself as a unity; it seems more akin to the animal than to the human consciousness; it is conscious but not self-conscious. In any case no statement about such a universal consciousness is a statement about individual survival of death. So far as human beings are concerned, the existence of the divine consciousness is as irrelevant to human destiny as is the materialist's whirl of energy-bundles.

Stace followed up this exposition of his thesis with the statement: "One now understands how the Hindu can assert that a soul . . . will be absorbed in God, and how this dissolution of personality will yet not be extinction."

But that is precisely what I do *not* understand. Stace offers us merely an assertion, not an explanation.

We must now briefly discuss the doctrine of reincarnation. It will be clear from the previous argument that the only evidence which could justify the affirmation that Jones in the twentieth century is identical with Brown in the seventeenth, is that Jones remembers the details of Brown's life in chronological sequence just as Brown remembered it just before he died. Anything less than this would be insufficient. For example, Jones might have recurring dreams about people in seventeenth-century costumes, but this would be very far from what is needed; there might be many alternative explanations. It is important in this connection to notice that cases of children "remembering" past lives seem to be commoner in lands where reincarnation is taught than elsewhere. The psychological explanation is probably similar to that of the fact that Christian children brought up in evangelical homes quite sincerely experience "conversion" more commonly than children brought up in Catholic households.

But a claim by anyone to remember past existence must not, in such a serious matter, be taken at its face value. There is no question of imputing conscious insincerity, but the human mind is very complex, and we have not only the right, but the duty, to require corroborative evidence. We ought to be at least as meticulous as is the Society for Psychical Research when it scrutinizes claims to have received communications from the departed. Most people who declare their belief in reincarnation seem to have not the slightest idea of the amount and the kind of evidence needed to establish it. With regard to the *kind* of evidence, the same is true as of the spiritualists' claim that communications are from the departed; the required evidence will not be in the realm of religion or uplift—it will be a matter of very prosaic material details. If someone claims to remember living during the Commonwealth, and then tells us, for example, that he buried a box of jewellery in 1650 at a certain place, and if we then dig for it and find it, this will be *prima facie* evidence that he has some kind of super-normal knowledge, and reincarnation will then be one of the possible explanations. But actually there is very little evidence of this kind. The world-religions which teach reincarnation do so on moral or religious grounds. Let us examine these. But before doing so let us notice that these religions, as indeed did Christianity, ante-dated by a long period our scientific knowledge of the connection between nervous and mental process and of the biological laws of heredity. A man may re-produce his maternal grandfather's abnormal talent for mathematics and his father's "drive", or lack of it. The reincarnation and karma doctrines are difficult to fit in here. They derive from the crude animism which regards a soul as *inhabitating* a body, much as a dog inhabits a kennel. Just as the same dog can inhabit successively a series of kennels so the same spirit can inhabit successively a series of bodies, and there is as little organic connection between spirit and body as there is between dog and kennel. The modern awareness of the minute parallelism between nerve event and mental event renders such a conception untenable.

But cannot the reincarnation theory, and the doctrine of karma—the doctrine that a person is suffering in this life because of sins in a past one—be defended on religious and moral grounds?

Let us first notice that the natural and almost inevitable result of such a doctrine is to dry up the springs of human sympathy, even though those who first taught the doctrine did not intend this. We can argue this on *a priori* grounds, but there is factual evidence. There is a close connection between the system of caste in India and the doctrine of Karma. A man is born a Brahman as a reward for his past life, and born an outcaste as a punishment. Whether the teachers intend it or no, such a doctrine is bound to operate, and unquestionably has operated, as a justification of the caste system with all its evils. Arthur Koestler tells us[10] that the Oriental attitude to the sick and poor is "notoriously indifferent", because caste, rank, wealth and health are pre-ordained by the laws of karma. He adds that welfare work in the slums and care of the poor were (when he wrote) carried on almost exclusively by Christians. Gandhi acknowledged that his social enthusiasm was inspired by Christianity.

The notion of karma is based on a fallacy, namely that suffering as such is redemptive. It is not. The truth seems to be that suffering in itself does not make a person good, but that a person already good can so react to it as to become better. A punishment in itself has no moral value; it may indeed brutalize the offender, or make him defiant and bitter. Its moral value depends on his accepting it in the right spirit. But how can you acquiesce in being punished for a life which you do not remember leading and which, therefore, there is no reason for asserting to have been *your* life?

[10] *The Lotus and the Robot*, p. 280. Collins, 1960.

CHAPTER 6

Theology as Empirical Science

OUR CONSIDERATION of the two types of language in Chapter 2 opens up some most interesting questions. How, for example, are they related to each other and to the objective situation, and does the discovery of this relationship throw any light on the so-called body-mind problem? To discuss this further would be beyond the scope of this book; moreover, I have done so elsewhere.[1] Suffice to recall that we saw sound reasons for holding that we are discussing reality at a deeper level when we are using personal, psychological concepts than when we use concepts drawn from physical sciences.

Perhaps the most fundamental question that we can ask is whether we can trust our reasoning powers. For if we say "No" it is quite pointless to discuss any serious question. If we say "Yes" it would be absurd to try to find reasons for our decision, for this would be to assume the very thing to be proved, namely that we can trust our rational faculties. If some fiend has endowed us with reasoning powers which deceive us, any rational proof that we can trust our reasoning powers would be invalid. If, however, we venture on an act of faith in reason, no proof will have stronger grounds than our act of faith.

Now, if we trust our reasoning powers at all, we shall trust them when they make a distinction between what really is and

[1] *Christian Rationalism and Philosophical Analysis.* James Clarke and Co., 1959.

what merely *appears* to be, and we shall trust the most fundamental criteria which we all find ourselves using in deciding
between reality and mere appearance. To the extent that any
mental construction contains contradictions we say it cannot,
to that extent, be true; it cannot represent the real. One of the
formal characteristics of reality is consistency, or absence of
inner contradiction.

But there is another characteristic. If a particle at some
instant in its motion swerves from its previous path, we say
that there must have been a reason for this. We just cannot
believe that there was nothing to *make* it swerve. Moreover,
we cannot possibliy believe that sheer nothingness can change
into something—let alone into a highly organized something.
In other words, we have an intellectual instinct to believe that
if we can discover system and unity, and therefore simplicity,
in what formerly appeared chaotic and complicated, we are
seeing it more *as it really is* than we saw it before. Moreover,
we know that reality cannot be *objectively* mysterious. The
sense of mystery is a sign that what is before us is mere appearance. Things are mysterious *to us*, not *in themselves*. Words
like "mysterious" and "indefinite" are essentially subjective
words.

Now, if someone says that he mistrusts all these thought-
instincts, we can invite him to try to analyse his motives. Why
is he taking this line? Only because, I believe, he sees more or
less clearly where trust of the instincts may lead him, and does
not want to go! He cannot deny, for example, that the tre-
mendous advance of science has been inspired by a trust that
if only we seek diligently we shall find reasons or causes for
all changes, shall find system and unity. The trust has been
amply vindicated.

Now, the thesis that reality is basically mental or psychological or personal, and that it is a systematic consistent unity
and not, *in itself*, mysterious, has led philosophers to the conception of Reality as "The Absolute". In Chapter 2 we saw
sound reasons for believing that the real world which is, meta-

phorically speaking, "behind" our respective perceptual fields is not bare or abstract object, but Subject-with Object. We now combine this belief with our belief that the more we systematize and unify our thought-worlds, the more adequately they copy reality. The Absolute is thus conceived as actually realizing the ideal of a completely comprehensive and systematic awareness.

One great advantage of the concept of the Absolute over the concept of a dead abstract material world-in-itself, is that it justifies our belief that somehow *values*, moral and æsthetic, are objective. I can justify my belief that in holding that cruelty or that treachery is wrong, and not right, I am making as factual a statement as I am in holding that three sevens make twenty-one and not twenty-two. In both cases the human judgment is correct because it corresponds to Divine Judgment. (Incidentally, it is difficult to see how a human judgment could achieve truth-correspondence with anything except a Judgment.)

In saying that the Absolute or Divine Awareness actually realizes the ideal knowledge at which the human intellect implicitly aims, I am far from saying that finite minds—minds equipped with only the human thought-categories—are in principle capable of achieving the Absolute awareness. We can achieve a certain degree of unity within different fields—in physics or in biology or in psychology—but our minds are not capable of combining all these sectional unities into One Unity. We can achieve truths but not Truth. We shall explore this thought a little later.

The concept of the Absolute has aroused suspicion, and indeed hostility, amongst Christian philosophers and theologians. It is my belief that these suspicions are groundless, and that the concept of the Absolute is quite compatible with orthodox Christianity. I hope that what follows may help readers to see how this can be. I do not believe that Absolutism is necessarily pantheistic, and I hold it to be perfectly compatible with the Christian belief that human individuals can survive death as individuals. If belief in the Absolute is compatible with my awareness of myself as in this life an entity distinct from Jones, there is not the slightest reason why it should not equally be compatible in the next life. It is interesting in this connection to notice that although in the earlier writings of that great philosopher of the Absolute, F. H. Bradley, he tended to deprecate belief in the survival of human personality after death, he changed his attitude towards the end of his life. In 1923 he wrote as follows to Seth Pringle-Pattison, after reading the latter's Gifford lectures *The Idea of Immortality*, "I have seldom, if ever, read any book on such a subject which carried me with it so fully. . . . I certainly would *not* say now that a future life must be taken as decidedly improbable."[2]

But having stated my belief in the Absolute, I must hasten to add that our direct knowledge of the Absolute is quite bare and formal. In saying this I am not making a grudging admission but expressing a deep positive conviction. Religion needs far more than this formal knowledge. I believe that the bare and direct knowledge of the Absolute—knowledge arrived at by the kind of argument I have used—needs to be supplemented by an empirical study of the way the Absolute is revealed in the time-process. Christian theology is more akin to science than philosophy.

The empirical method is that method which we employ implicitly, i.e. without analysing it explicitly, in our everyday living and in science. When a countryman notices a general connection between red sky in the morning and rain he is using (correctly or incorrectly) the empirical method used by the physicist, the chemist and the biologist. As everyone knows, the great modern scientific advance began when men ceased to rely on deductions from so-called first principles and began to use the method of induction, i.e. they observed facts and then tried to think out some systematic, generalizing and unifying way of talking about what they saw. Now we rely, in the main,

[2] This letter is quoted on page 145 of a memoir on Pringle-Pattison prefaced to his *Balfour Lectures on Realism*. Blackwood, 1933.

on this empirical method in arriving at our religious or theological beliefs.

But I have just written "in the main". For all empirical thinking, scientific or theological, takes place, so to speak, inside a metaphysical framework. Whenever we use empirical language—for example, when we speak of verifying a hypothesis—we are picturing our subject matter against a background. Or, to change the figure, we are using a model. The study of these backgrounds or models is metaphysics. For example, when we are doing mechanics or chemistry, we have as our background or model a vast objective space and a vast objective time, within which framework there function bits of matter or energy or waves. That this is a metaphysical model is seen from the fact that some of the greatest metaphysicians —and indeed some of the mathematical physicists—have seriously questioned it. But normally, when we are being scientists, we just *assume* the background. If you ask a scientist how did the bits of matter or energy-bundles—or the space-time framework itself—come to be, he will probably reply that this is not a scientific question. He may venture on some kind of answer, but he will tell you that he is not now speaking as a scientist.

Some people to whom you asked such a question would say, "That is a metaphysical question, *and therefore unanswerable*." A few years ago that attitude was commoner and more confident than it is today. One thing is certain. It is not self-evident that metaphysics is just waste of time—that we can say nothing useful about "ultimate" questions. The only person entitled to be heard with respect on the subject is the person who has studied both metaphysics and modern philosophical analysis very deeply.

The most obvious difference between scientific and metaphysical questions is that a scientific doctrine can—at any rate in principle—be falsified by the observation of some particular fact or facts. But there are some questions which we instinctively ask, which we find fascinating, and the answers to which may well affect our conduct, but since they are concerned with a *general* way of talking—a way of talking about all facts of a certain type—they cannot be answered by observation of any particular facts. These are the metaphysical questions. For example, there is the problem of law versus chance. At one extreme we may find someone holding that the rarest kind of events—or even a unique event—must be due to a law. At the other extreme it would be possible, without self-contradiction, to hold that the most regular sequences of events, even those which we account for by appealing to the law of gravitation, are merely a run of luck, like a penny falling heads a hundred times running. If anyone held either view, he could not be confuted by any experiment. They would both be metaphysical views, the first of which is perfectly feasible while the second seems fantastic.

There are, then, legitimate and significant questions which are general and formal, and with which the scientist as such, is not concerned. Conversely there are questions with which the philosopher as such is not concerned. These include scientific questions, which can be decided only by the empirical method—by observation and by what is at first hypothesis but which, if it escapes falsification long enough, we regard as a "law". Now, when we are studying religion and theology we are concerned with both these types of question. Firstly, we ask whether there are any formal or general statements which we can make about the Absolute. Secondly, we use the empirical method and ask whether there are any generalizations warranted by experience, i.e. in principle falsifiable but actually verified by observation, which we can reasonably claim to reveal what in our anthropomorphic way we must regard as the "workings" or "purposes" in time, in history, of this Absolute Mind.

We have, in effect, defined the word "reality" as the-Universe-as-the-Absolute-Mind-knows-it. But we must not make the mistake of describing whatever is not reality-awareness as error or illusion. We have to make a three-fold division. Firstly, knowledge of Reality which only the Absolute possesses. Secondly, human truth. Thirdly, human error. Human truth consists of (1) the formal, true statements which human beings can make about the Absolute Mind. (2) Our everyday, and our scientific, true statements based on observation. (3) True statements in empirical theology.

I have already outlined the kind of bare, formal knowledge about the Absolute's awareness, or Reality-awareness, which human beings can have. I here wish to draw out an implication of the fact that the Absolute's awareness, although it includes ours, includes it in such a context as to solve our mysteries. To be aware of infinite time and space, in the way that we finite beings are aware, is to be confronted with mystery. But awareness of mystery is essentially subjective; the mysterious is what merely appears to be, not what really is. The Absolute awareness, which is the awareness of reality, therefore transcends *our* time and space awareness.

We can also see that, from our definition, the Absolute is not confronted with "external" brute facts as we are. All the objects of His awareness must be expressions of what we must, anthropomorphically, call His Will.

But this is about as far as we can go in the way of formal metaphysical knowledge of the Absolute. We can say that all problems are solved, all questions answered, in the Absolute Mind. In itself this is insufficient for religion, but it is necessary to it. For without belief in an Actual Awareness which realizes our ideal of a perfect knowledge, the interpretation of an empirical study of the ethical and religious consciousness by language about "God" is unwarranted. A *purely* empirical theology would have as little right as has any empirical science to pronounce on ultimate problems. Most scientists see, and frankly admit, the limitations of their particular science, but theologians who repudiate metaphysics are curiously blind.

We can now consider the possibility of an empirical theology within a framework of bare metaphysical concepts, a theology which will be, as it were, parallel to the empirical sciences which also, as we have seen, assume a metaphysical background. We have noticed that the distinction between human truth and human error is a quite different distinction from that between the Divine or Absolute Awareness, on the one hand, and human awareness (whether true or false) on the other. All our human experience takes place, so to speak, in a framework of time and space. The Divine awareness somehow—in a way quite beyond our comprehension—transcends this.

I can now explain what I mean by "empirical theology". A physicist, chemist or biologist might justly say, "My concern, as scientist, is not directly with the X which we all postulate as somehow behind phenomena, but solely with observing how this X is revealed in empirically discovered laws in the time-and-space-framework". Now, the Christian theologian can say something very similar to this. He need not—indeed, in my view he *should* not—agree that the X is *quite* unknowable except as revealed in time; we can, and need to, claim formal knowledge of X—enough to insist that the pronoun "He" is more appropriate than the pronoun "It"; but we can agree that for the practical, the conduct-affecting knowledge which theology seeks, and for the satisfying of the hunger which inspires the religious quest, we must use methods akin to those of science—empirical methods; we must appeal to moral and religious experience.

This leads to a point of an importance impossible to exaggerate. Just as the scientist will tell us that he is concerned not with X in itself, but with how X is revealed in the laws governing phenomena in time and space, so the Christian can, and indeed must, say that religion is concerned not with speculations about God the Absolute, God in His utter transcendence, God-in-and-for-Himself, but with God as revealed in concrete events in the time process—God in history and in religious and moral experience. Here we must remember that, as Aristotle pointed out long ago, the nature of a process is far better revealed by its later than by its earlier stages. To know trends we must know ends. It is therefore rational to look for God's greatest revelation of himself in the study of *human* history and human inner experience. Nor need we confine ourselves to a search for general laws. There is no reason why God should not reveal Himself in particular events.

We have only to use the term "God the Father", meaning God the ultimate source of all, for the Absolute, and "God the Son or Logos or Word", or even "the Eternal Christ", for God as revealed in the time process, to see that we are approaching the Christian doctrine of the Incarnation.

Once we see that Christian theology partakes of the nature of empirical science, we have a sufficient answer to anyone who points out that it has loose ends, and does not offer a tidy scheme. For in this it exactly resembles the physical sciences. It is concerned, like them, with human truths. It can never in the nature of things attain that all-inclusive omniscience, that entire transcendence of mystery which characterizes the Absolute's awareness. Theology sorts out human truths from human errors in the same way, fundamentally, as do the other empirical sciences, and the theologian has just as much right as has the scientist, when he is asked "ultimate" questions, to say that his science does not profess to answer them. His concern, like theirs, is to describe what happens—to do so in general terms when generalizations, and even the enunciation of general laws, are possible, but otherwise to describe particulars accurately.

For example, if you point out to the physicist that sometimes he explains the transmission of light as if it were particles and sometimes as if it were waves, and that he does not offer a single picture which accounts for all phenomena, he will reply somewhat as follows: The wave picture as a whole is true in the sense that it accounts for certain of our sense experiences and enables us successfully to predict the future course of certain kinds of experience; the particle picture similarly accounts for other sense experiences and enables us successfully to predict other types of event. We need not withhold the word "true" because we cannot fit the particular picture we are using into an overall picture of complete consistency and coherence, nor because our science begins by taking a lot for granted and not trying to explain how the whole system started. The theologian's answer will be similar, except that he is talking not of sense-experiences but of moral and religious experiences.

Now, just as the natural sciences have their basic concepts —energy, elementary particles, waves, force, quanta, entropy, growth, and so on—so does theology. An important basic concept of Christian theology, as we have seen, is that the Absolute God, the "Father", is revealed in history as God-the-Son. All our concrete statements which represent God as acting in the time series are about God-the-Son. And once we have grasped the distinction between the Absolute God's Awareness and even our truest beliefs—between Truth and Reality on the one hand and truths on the other—we shall as little expect to achieve a completely luminous picture with no dark patches as does the natural scientist. But the distinction between human truth and human falsity will remain as sharp as it is in physics; we shall reject some doctrines offered us because certain experiences falsify them; we shall suspend belief in others because we cannot see how they are verified; we shall accept others with confidence because they fit the facts.

With this in mind, let us consider the problem of evil and suffering. Let us begin by asking how God-the-Father could be revealed in the time series as good; in other words how can God-the-Son be experienced as good. It is obvious that the concept of goodness as distinct from innocence presupposes the concept of evil, sorrow and pain. Only in the world as we know it could goodness as we know it exist. Moreover, if we think of God-the-Son as working in the time-process, we must think of Him as having purposes, which he achieves *gradually*—think of Him as using means to ends, as being opposed and hindered, *and therefore as suffering*. The overcoming of opposites, in dialectical process, is of the essence of God's time-revelation. He is revealed in goodness fighting evil, order imposing itself on chaos, wisdom hindered and limited by human stupidity. It seems to be of the essence of finite knowledge that we should see reality dialectically, i.e. see it as thesis and antithesis, whether in natural science, psychology or theology. William James long ago insisted that Hegel was not so much a metaphysician as a superb empiricist; you can see thesis and antithesis everywhere. I would add that it seems to be of the essence of finitude to see reality thus; only the Absolute, the Father, can know the synthesis.

The empirical theologian's answer to the old question why a good God put evil and pain into the world He had made—or permitted it to enter—is that we reject this whole picture. We no longer occupy the standpoint which the wording of the question betrays. It is the wrong kind of mythology—not even human truth, let alone the standpoint of reality-awareness. We must get the question right before we can attempt an answer. This will involve an enquiry into the limitations of human thought. Such an enquiry has actually been conducted by philosophers—Kant for example—not as an *ad hoc* attempt to solve the problem before us but because of its intrinsic interest and importance. When we have done this, we reject as childish the myth of an anthropomorphic God "making" a world at a moment of time like a carpenter making a box, and putting, or permitting someone else to put, evil into it as articles might be put into a box. We can say about God only what we can say about God-the-Son, God as revealed in time fighting evil. You cannot have a consistent and therefore a humanly true picture of God as both fighting and making, or even both fighting and permitting, evil. Our theology is an empirical ethical dualism against a background of a purely formal monism.

"But in that case," you may say, "why do you insist that the Absolute is revealed by one rather than the other side of the dualism? Why by the good rather than by the bad?" The answer of an empirical theology is that the facts point that way. There is that vast consensus of conviction, starting from

I

the Hebrew prophets, for example (to say nothing of Greek and other ethical religions), that God has revealed Himself, to those that seek Him, as good. Again, as we saw in Chapter 3, an analysis of the moral conscience, made with a willingness to accept it for what it is and not to explain it away, leaves us with a belief that moral values must in some sense be objective, and it is far easier to fit such a belief into theism than into materialism or pantheism.

Again, we can point to the fact that we believe God's awareness to achieve that complete systematic unity which is, for the human thinker, only a far-off ideal. One of the outstanding characteristics of the good life is that it has a unity which the bad life lacks. Goodness is associated in our minds with order, system and unity, whereas the life of a bad man, if rich and complex, displays considerable inner conflict, and if free from conflict, achieves such freedom by excluding vast ranges of experience. We can consistently think therefore, of a vast, comprehensive *and harmonious* experience as good. Moreover, it is easier to account for evil in a basically moral universe than to account for the emergence of the categorical imperative by chance in an immoral or non-moral universe. Admittedly, no serious thinker claims to have completely solved the mystery of evil when he notices that real goodness can exist only in a world where there is evil and pain. But equally no honest thinker can deny the vital importance of this curious fact, or can resist the feeling that somehow this is the main clue.

The theologian can reasonably claim to have found in his field a vast generalization comparable to Newton's law of gravitation in the field of physics. He uses the concept of purpose as science uses any of its basic categories. He tries to see all the relevant facts steadily and to see them whole, and he says that the purpose of human life, whether men recognize it or not, is the emergence of moral character—although even this is not a final end, an end-in-itself. "Blessed are the pure in heart, *for they shall see God*". This earth, then, is for men a vale of soul-making. This is the only way of making sense of life. You can, of course, be content that life shall *not* make sense. But this, as we saw in Chapter 3, is to make a fundamental moral commitment. Men can love darkness rather than the light.

CHAPTER 7

The Eternal Son and the Historical Jesus

AMONG THE passages recording or referring to the life of Jesus in the New Testament there are some which portray him as simply human. In Peter's speech at Pentecost Jesus is "a man approved of God unto you by mighty works and wonders and signs which God did by him"—a man whom God had raised up and exalted to His right hand. In *Luke* we read that the child Jesus increased in wisdom and stature. In *Mark* we read that he prayed "Not what I will but what thou wilt" and that he even refused to be called "good" on the ground that God alone was good. There is no need to read guilt-consciousness into this last; it was the belief of a pious Jew that goodness was essentially a Divine attribute and that human goodness was somehow a *derived* goodness; but it does portray Jesus as regarding himself on the human side of the gulf which Jewish orthodoxy put between God and man. Many other passages bearing the same implication could be quoted.

There are, however, other passages in which Jesus is regarded as Messiah, Son of God, or Son of Man. And some scholars believe that he even felt himself called upon to fulfil the Isaian prophecy of the Suffering Servant. Do any of these descriptions lift him out of the ranks of humanity? Certainly not that of political Messiah; those who used that concept conceived of the Messiah as a human being—a man called to fulfil a certain function. And whether Jesus regarded himself, or came to be regarded by his disciples after the Resurrection, as Son of Man, this concept would again be that of a created being—a being either already given, or else due to be given later on, a very high function but one far short of Divine. The title "Son of God" again, as used by orthodox Jews, would be quite compatible with full humanity; it was metaphor, nor metaphysic; any good or important man might be called son or child of God. And the Suffering Servant, if regarded as an individual, would be regarded as a human individual. Passages applying any of these four concepts to Jesus do not, then, necessarily fall outside the group of passages describing Jesus as a purely human being.

It has often been said that orthodox Judaism put a vast gulf between men and God—between, in fact, all created beings and God—and that it was only in the pagan world that the distinction between humanity and divinity was blurred. But it has become less clear than it once seemed that even in Palestine, in the time of Christ, Jewish thought was unanimously "pure", i.e. free from pagan influence in this matter. It is important to bear this in mind when we come to consider a third group of passages which differ from the first and second groups in that they portray Jesus as more than human. For an explanation of the occurrence of this third group will readily occur to anyone acquainted with the thought of the ancient pagan world, namely that they witness to a process, by no means uncommon, of "apotheosis"—the ascription of divine attributes to a human being after his death. Now those who wish in this way to account for the third group of passages found it necessary in the past to show that the apotheosis was due to the spread of the faith into the pagan world, and that it must, therefore, have occurred after some lapse of time; they assumed, that is, that it could not have taken place while the new faith was confined to Palestine itself, where pure and rigid monotheism prevailed everywhere. But if, as we now suspect, Palestinian religion at that time was not quite universally monotheistic in the strictest sense, then some kind of apotheosis of Jesus could have taken place quite early and in Palestine. The mere fact, then, that a document is early and Jewish does not prove that it contains an authentic picture of the teachings of Jesus about himself; it *could* be an apotheosis.

The view that Palestinian thought at the time of Jesus was not unanimous in its adherence to the clear-cut monotheism of the prophets has emerged from the study of the Dead Sea Scrolls and the Nag Hammadi documents. It has been shown that there was a sort of embryonic gnosticism in the life and literature of the Essenes and near-Essenes of the Qumran community; indeed gnosticism had some of its roots in apocalyptic Judaism.[1] There are parallels between the Scrolls and the Fourth Gospel. But this was only one element in the mosaic of Johannine theology; there were others—Philo for example and later forms of thought expressed in the Hermetic literature. These imply a later date for the Fourth Gospel.

The old view, indeed, of the apotheosis of Jesus as being due to the spread of the faith into the pagan world has by no means been discredited. It is by no means clear that the paganization of Judaism affected anything more than the outer fringe of Palestinian thought. It certainly looks, from early Acts and from much in the synoptic gospels, that the early disciples had a fairly simple and orthodox creed. In the eyes of the first Jewish Christians Jesus was a man who had been called upon by God to be Son-of-Man; he had been crucified, but he had ascended to heaven and was soon coming again.

The mere fact, then, if it is a fact, that some of the conceptions in the Fourth Gospel could have originated in Palestine and at an early date, is no proof that they actually did. The case for regarding the Fourth Gospel as a late and extra-Palestinian work is based on a vast array of evidence. The external evidence, for example, is quite untouched by recent speculations about Palestinian thought. It is set out very forcibly in B. W. Bacon's *The Fourth Gospel in Research and Debate*, and this detailed argument has never, in my view, been refuted. F. C. Grant, in *The Gospels, their Origins and Growth*,[2] decidedly

---

[1] R. M. Grant, *Gnosticism and Early Christianity*. O.U.P., 1959.
[2] Faber, 1959.

rejects the suggestion that in view of certain parallels in the Dead Sea Scrolls the Fourth Gospel must have been written in purely Jewish circles at an early date; he dates the gospel early in the second century.

Examples of passages in the third group—passages which describe Jesus as more than human—include the passages in which Paul describes Jesus as a pre-existent being who came down to earth to redeem mankind, and also those in the Fourth Gospel in which Jesus is represented as claiming pre-existence and divinity: "Before Abraham was, I am". Many Christian scholars hold, and I think they are right, that passages which describe Jesus as pre-existent, including the Johannine ones in which he is regarded as having himself claimed pre-existence, are to be explained as the fruits of meditation; they are theology, not history; the historical Jesus did not "claim to be God". There is no need to elaborate the point here; a vast literature exists on the subject, and it would be difficult to say anything fresh. I will merely call attention to a simple consideration. If the historical Jesus had taught his disciples the Christology of the Nicene Creed it is difficult to account for the first group of passages to which I have referred. I am not here being heterodox; scholars of unimpeachable orthodoxy agree that the full Christian Christology, although a valid implication of the fact of Jesus, needed time to develop. But there is less difficulty in explaining the genesis of the third group of passages if the first group is authentic. Indeed, the difficulty is not in finding an explanation; it is, rather, in the choosing between a number of possible ones. In Hebrew thought there had been a semi-personification of Wisdom, and this invited comparison with the Greek Logos. There is evidence, too, that even in the first century those speculations had already begun which later were to produce the so-called mystery religions and the various gnostic theosophies, with ideas of saviour-gods. All this tended to blur the clear-cut distinction which the prophets had put between Creator and creature; the pagan tendency was to attribute divine qualities to men and human qualities to the gods.

In the twentieth century we must reject much of this pagan speculation and criticize carefully the whole movement of thought which resulted in the language of the creeds of Nicea and Chalcedon. But this is very far from saying, "Let us reject all of it and get back to a simple human Jesus." A hasty sweeping aside of a vast and widespread movement of human thought, which must have expressed deep-seated human instincts, would be foolish. Why need we suppose that the *praeparatio evangelica* was, in the Divine providence, being made only in Palestine; why not in the pagan world as well? And to say, "Let us get back to the simple human Jesus", is to assume the very thing to be proved or disproved. *Was* Jesus "merely human"? Is *any* good man merely human? However grim the truth may prove to be, we shall face it if we have to, but let us make no mistake: there is no gospel in the assertion that a good man called Jesus was martyred. I believe that it is an oversimplification—indeed it is false—to say that Jesus was a mere man. It is one thing to say that orthodox Jews put a gulf between creature and Creator, and that this was nice and simple and ethical; it is quite another to say that they were right. The transcendence of God is only one side of the truth; the immanence of God, distorted though it be by pagan myth and gnostic fantasy, is equally vital.

Let us be clear on one essential point. Our attempt to evaluate the process of meditation on the fact of Jesus which culminated in the historic creeds is distinct from the historical question of his "claims"—if any—about himself. Dr. Leonard Hodgson has given the weight of his authority to the statement, "It is not necessary to faith in the godhead of Christ to maintain that during his earthly life he was consciously aware of that godhead."[3]

The question of the content of the self-consciousness of Jesus is an outstanding example of that uncertainty which so often confronts us in our study of Christian origins—an uncertainty which indicates that no view of the self-consciousness of Jesus

[3] *The Doctrine of the Atonement*, p. 138.

can be an essential element in the Christian Kerygma—the Gospel Proclamation. We can broadly distinguish three views. (1) The Fourth Gospel is correct in attributing to Jesus a knowledge of his pre-existence as Divine Logos. (2) On the contrary, he thought of himself as on the human side of the gulf which, in the eyes of orthodox Jews, separated God from men, but that he believed himself to be called by God to be Son of Man and/ or Suffering Servant. (3) He did not even believe himself to be Son of Man or Suffering Servant. The support of distinguished Christian scholars can be claimed for each of these three theses.

On the question whether Jesus regarded his death as redemptive there is not, I think, room for much uncertainty. It seems clear that Jesus did not regard his death as the necessary means whereby individual men could be forgiven. A vast array of passages from the Old Testament could be quoted, and Jesus must have known them, in which it was clearly taught that the sole essential condition for the forgiveness of sin was sincere repentance. The parables of the Prodigal Son, the Pharisee and the Publican, the Lost Sheep, and the Lost Coin—and, of course, the Lord's Prayer—make it clear that Jesus accepted this Old Testament teaching. But it also seems probable that *in some sense* Jesus regarded his death as redemptive. Indeed, some of the best minds in his nation and day had begun to wonder whether the voluntary self-sacrifice of God's servants could not be used by God for His redemptive purposes for the Jewish *nation*. In II Maccabees vii, vv. 37–38 we read, "But I, as my brethren, give up both body and soul for the laws of our fathers, calling upon God that He may speedily become propitious to the nation . . . and that in me and my brethren may be stayed the wrath of the Almighty." Jesus may well have conceived of his coming death as redemptive *of the nation*—in an "apocalyptic" sense; he may well have regarded himself as ushering in a New Age in which God's plan for Israel would be manifest.

But I must reject, as due to bias or to the natural tendency to over-state a new theory, the attempt of certain critics obsessed with apocalyptic to represent the outlook of Jesus as primarily apocalyptic and only incidentally ethical. The ethic of Jesus was by no means merely an interim-ethic. And he not only taught it; he lived it; it was the moral grandeur of his personality that drew men to him. In particular, I must dissent from the attempt to represent Jesus as in sympathy with the Zealot movement—and especially from the view that he could not have been truly good unless he had been at heart a Zealot. Nationalism—whether German or British or Jewish—is an evil. All the evidence shows that his apocalyptic took the form of a belief that the Jews ought to prepare themselves, by repentance alone, for a *Divine* event. You cannot argue that he must have sympathized with the Zealots because someone is reported to have drawn a sword when he was arrested!

In rejecting the view that Jesus "claimed to be God" we are not rejecting the Christian doctrine of the Incarnation. In this connection we must remember that the Church has condemned as heresy the view of Apollinaris that only the body and the sensory life of Jesus were human and that his "nous"—the spiritual and rational element in his consciousness—was purely Divine. The orthodox view is that Jesus had a completely human nature. The Church was right in condemning Apollinarianism, but it has shown a curious reluctance to face the implications of its action. The uniqueness of Jesus did not lie in his being metaphysically different in kind from other men; he was unique in that because he lived and died and lived again mankind achieved that full self-consciousness which is also God-consciousness.

We shall never grasp the essential truth of the Incarnation so long as we feel the issue to be academic or theoretical. It is the Answer to the Question compared with which all others are trivial. If a man has looked up, in sadness and perhaps in bitterness, at the silent stars with their mocking impersonality, and has asked whether there is any purpose in the system which has produced them and him, then he is at least on the way to realizing what is at stake in this matter of the Incarnation. We cannot ascribe Purpose unless in some sense we can ascribe something akin to Mind. Now we saw in Chapter 2 that the postulation of cosmic Mind is not just wishful thinking but has rational grounds. But the question remains—is the nature of this Mind revealed only in infinite vastness, and in the infinite rationality which there must be since science is possible? Browning surely goes to the heart of the matter in his *Saul*.

> "'Tis the weakness in strength that I cry for! my flesh, that
>   I seek
> In the Godhead! I seek and I find it. O Saul, it shall be
> A Face like my face that receives thee: a Man like to me,
> Thou shalt love and be loved by, for ever! a Hand like
>   this hand
> Shall throw open the gates of new life to thee! See the
>   Christ stand!"

The Hebrew prophets believed that man was made "in God's image". The Christian faith is the working out in logic and in history of this insight. Because Jesus lived, men came to believe that there is humanity in God. As we saw in the last chapter, our knowledge of God as the Source of all is but formal, but we can know God-as-revealed-in-history, God-the-Son. Because of Jesus we can believe that the picture of man at his highest is the truest picture we can have of God-the-Son.

It was vital to a revelation of the essential truth of the doctrine of the Incarnation that Jesus should be seen to be fully human. That was why the Church rightly condemned Apollinarianism. But the pagan notions which inspired that heresy have been hard to kill. In the twentieth century we must insist that if there is a point of identity between divinity and humanity so that one and the same person could be both human and divine, then complete divinity and complete humanity must be affirmed. To water down either concept is to dodge the issue. A person whose human knowledge and power were unlimited and who remembered pre-existence as Logos would not be human at all. The unique divinity of Jesus is established for us not because he "claimed to be God" and had a unique sense of divinity, for we have no clear evidence of such a claim or such a sense, but because of his unique moral character and his unique place in history.

The essence of the Hebrew and Christian conception of God is seen by contrasting it with the conceptions of God found among Greek and Oriental religious thinkers. Metaphysically, it was the Hebrews who put a gulf between men and God, whereas much Greek and Oriental thinking tended to blur the distinction.

It might almost be said that in Hebrew and Christian thought God was ontologically transcendent and ethically immanent—immanent in human goodness—whereas in much Graeco-Oriental thought God was ontologically immanent and ethically transcendent—beyond good and evil. It is quite consistent with this distinction that in the pagan and pantheistic view men realize God only by transcending their everyday rational, moral and self-conscious experience and entering a trance-state in which they share the Divine life and transcend all distinctions—even that of good and evil. Those of us, however, who accept the Hebrew and Christian view, hold that we can trust our reason, and our everyday self-conscious experience of ourselves as individuals. And above all, God is *not* beyond good and evil; He is revealed in the human conscience at its highest, far more than by trance-experiences. God is best known to us in an experience open to common people—not merely to mystics—an experience of genuine goodness in action, as seen pre-eminently in Jesus but also in all men and women who have fought against evil and suffered in the process.

The academic mind will want to ask whether, when we talk of God's being revealed to us in Jesus, or revealed in human life at its highest, we are asserting sheer identity on the one hand or merely similarity on the other. I have discussed this issue elsewhere, so I do not propose to discuss it here.[4] It will suffice here to say that in my view the concept of identity-in-difference as developed by the so-called neo-Hegelian philosophers—a concept which points the way to the reconciliation of the monism which our intellects demand with the plurality which we observe—is the key to the solution of this profound problem. Points of similarity between finite and infinite consciousness *are* points of identity. There *is* identity between Divinity and humanity-as-such; and when a perfect life was lived on earth the area of identity was extended so that in him dwelt all the fullness of the Godhead—in so far as humanity can hold it.

But I do not think that simple Christians—that any of us so far as our devotional life is concerned—need go into these abstrusenesses. For all practical purposes it comes to the same thing whether we say that God-the-Son was identical with, or whether we say that He was similar to, Jesus of Nazareth. What I need to know is how God will treat me, and so far as *that* is concerned it makes no difference whether I say that God was incarnate in Jesus, revealed Himself in Jesus, inspired Jesus or was like Jesus. For in any case He will treat me as Jesus would have done; that is all I need to know.

The modern philosophical approach, with its determination not to carry speculation to a point where distinctions can make no difference in practice—where they can make no difference *to us*—leads to the removal of a vast amount of dead wood from theology. For example, we can state the doctrine of the Trinity very simply, without the technicalities of fourth-century metaphysics—*ousia, hypostases, personae* or *prosopa.* As I have pointed out, the self is the only substance in its own right, so to speak, and just as a man can be one man and yet be father, lawyer and cricketer, so in our human way we can

---

[4] *God, Man and the Absolute.* Hutchinson, 1947. See also pages 121 to 123 of *Christian Rationalism and Philosophical Analysis.* James Clarke & Co., 1959. The concept of identity-in-difference is quite compatible with that of individual immortality. For if it is compatible with individual self-awareness in this earthly life, it is compatible with it in the future life.

think of God as (1) God-in-Himself, the almost unknowable Absolute—the *Father;* (2) God the Son, God as revealed in human history, as one with and active in all good men and pre-eminently with and in Jesus; (3) God as immanent in our think-ing—God as inspiring our true insights and giving us "grace" or power to over-come evil. If you say that (2) and (3) overlap, so do Son and Spirit in the New Testament. "The Lord *is* that Spirit". (II Cor. iii, 17.)

Similarly with the doctrine of the Atonement. The modern man's difficulty with "explanations" of the Atonement which belong to the mythology of the first Christian centuries is not merely that we cannot "understand" them, or are shocked by their crudity, but that we cannot see how any actual or obtain-able human experience could verify or falsity them; to that extent most of us are sufficiently positivistic in our outlook to feel them meaningless. How *could* we test the thesis that by the death of Jesus certain evil powers which held mankind in thrall were defeated? How *could* we test the thesis that the death of Jesus did on a cosmic scale what primitive peoples thought was done on a small scale when animals were sacri-ficed to appease the wrath of a diety?

The view which the modern man can find both intelligible and verifiable is the view which sees the Atonement in the light of the Incarnation. The Old Testament consistently portrayed God as a forgiving God, and our Lord's parables were in line with this. The sole condition for forgiveness was *genuine* repen-tance—a hatred of the sin and not merely a fear of punishment. There was no question of an Atonement being necessary in order that forgiveness might be possible; what was needed was a gospel which would make repentance genuine—not a change in God's attitude to men but a change in men's attitude to God. The truth of this psychological explanation of the Atonement can be verified; it *has* been verified; the gospel of the cross has changed innumerable lives. In Paul's words (Rom. ii, 4) the goodness of God has led them to repentance; they have felt that love so amazing has demanded their all.

One question remains to be discussed. How far is the historic Jesus vital to the Christian Faith? Supposing, it may be asked, that someone who has never heard of Jesus has arrived, by *whatever* process of experience or thought, at the deep conviction that the truest picture of God is that of a man who has lived and died in the service of men. And suppose this person tried, humbly and prayerfully, to follow this ideal, would he not be all that a Christian can be? We can suppose that he imagines as his ideal man someone exactly *like* Jesus, and that he sees in actual human vicarious suffering a revelation of the heart of God; we can further suppose that, just like a Christian, he regards salvation and eternal life as God's free gift, and does not claim to merit it. Would he not have been "born again", in the essentially Christian sense?

Now one answer would be that it could not happen. I could concede this without conceding my main point. I could concede, that is, that in fact no one would ever have had such a faith in God unless there had taken place that long process of Divine revelation recorded in the Bible. But one could still maintain that the details of the life of the historical Jesus— the fact that his name was "Jesus" and that he lived in Palestine 1900 years ago—are *in a sense* not essential. In the case of pure mathematics, for example, it is conceivable that had not some particular genius been born—a Newton or a Leibnitz—certain propositions which the average student can now prove for himself would never have been discovered. But since the proof can now be carried out by undergraduates who know nothing of the history of mathematics, neither of these great men is essential to the proof.

There is, then, no contradiction between holding that Christian theology would never have been historically possible unless God had revealed Himself in Jesus, and holding that Christianity is a philosophy or a rational theology, and can be expounded and defended as such. In announcing the Christian kerygma, we can affirm both that it is a historical revelation and that it has a solid basis in reason and experience.

Can we, then, regard the historical revelation in Jesus as the ladder by which men in fact rose to the true Faith, but which they can now kick away? In one sense we can say "Yes!"— in the sense, that is, in which St. Paul declared that we are no longer concerned with "Christ after the flesh". But misunderstanding is easy here. There has been a type of argument in certain neo-Calvinist circles which seems to amount to the thesis that while it is vital to hold that God broke into history in the person of a particular individual at a particular time, and wrought redemption through that person's death and resurrection, that is all we need to know. We are not concerned with his human psychology—with his ethical teaching or with, in fact, anything about him except that God performed His mighty acts through him.

This extreme view has not convinced most Christian theologians. It is compatible with belief in the Atonement only if we conceive of the Atonement as a mysterious objective transaction on which analogies from the counting-house or the law-courts can throw light. But the more closely we connect the Atonement with the Incarnation, and the more closely we connect the Incarnation with the ethical appeal which Jesus makes to us, the more we shall want to know about his teaching and his life. Here I believe modern critical methods to be of the greatest value. We shall be acutely aware that those who wrote the records of his life were, ethically and spiritually, far below him. We shall make allowance for the tendency of participants in early church controversies to edit his sayings in support of their contentions. But I believe that when criticism has done its work with complete honesty, an authentic picture remains of One who shames us all by his utter selflessness, his love for his fellows and his surrender to the will of God.

CHAPTER 8

Psychical Research and Christian Eschatology

PSYCHICAL RESEARCH is pre-eminently a field in which speculation as to antecedent probabilities is futile. Oddly enough,
there is no field of inquiry which people approach with more
initial bias. To be intellectually honest about it seems to require
a sustained effort which few people appear to make. I will first
consider some of the reasons for the strong prejudice against
it in many quarters.

In spite of the appearance of such outstanding works as
G. N. M. Tyrrell's *The Personality of Man* (Pelican) there is still
a tendency to confuse the scientific study of para-normal
phenomena with the cult of spiritualism. But here I must myself guard against bias—against a temptation to commend
psychical research by being unfair to spiritualists.

The general prejudice against spiritualism takes the form,
first, of a feeling that there is something unhealthy about it. We
must not dismiss this feeling as mere prejudice; but neither, on
the other hand, ought we to yield to it without some attempt
to analyse it and account for it; it may well prove groundless.

There can be little doubt that all who accept the Bible as in
any way authoritative tend to think of the mediumistic trance
in terms of the story of the witch of Endor. But those of us
who interpret the Bible as a record of a *progressive* revelation
will realize that the story, as it comes down to us, is coloured
by conceptions which we are not bound to accept. The early
thinking of the ancient Greeks and Hebrews about the state of

K

the departed, in *Hades* or in *Sheol*, does not yield a consistent and coherent picture; primitive people do not bother much about consistency. The departed were often imagined as having some kind of shadowy, gloomy existence from which endless sleep would be a happy release. But even those who attained such sleep were not secure in it; they were at the mercy of evil persons on earth who could "call them up". This is the background of the Endor story. Samuel says to Saul, "Why hast thou disquieted me, to bring me up?"

The task of dating the books of Samuel—and, in fact, most of the Old Testament writings—is not a simple one. They seem to have been the result of editorial work upon more ancient sources. It is, therefore, impossible to be sure that we have an accurate record of the words actually spoken if and when Saul consulted a witch. The account as we have it is almost certainly an interpretation in the light of the outlook of the times.

All enlightened modern thinkers must feel difficulties over this Hades-Sheol conception. The agnostic will feel sceptical over the whole business; the Christian will feel it impossible to believe that the blessed dead regard unbroken sleep—security from being "called up"—as the goal of existence. Above all, Jews and Christians will be well aware that even before the time of Christ the clearer thinkers and the nobler minds among the Hebrews had come to see the contradiction between affirming the goodness of Jehovah and his failure to vindicate the suffering righteous, and had come to believe in the resurrection to *life* as the destiny of the good man. The souls of the righteous were in the hand of God, and the idea that they were liable to be, as it were, dragged back to earth against their will, became incredible.

This particular objection, then, against the study of the mediumistic trance cannot be sustained. If it should prove true that, in certain circumstances, the departed can communicate with their friends on earth, it must be because they want to, and because God allows them to. It need hardly be added that spiritualists claim that there is abundant evidence that some, at any rate, of the departed are *anxious* to communicate with their friends on earth.

There are some people who are content to say that they have an instinctive dislike for the whole business of para-normal research. But can they be sure that their feeling *is* instinctive—if by that they mean that it was inborn and not acquired early in life? One's disgust at the suggestion that one should eat a rat *seems* instinctive, but we quite cheerfully eat another form of rodent—a rabbit. It is very doubtful whether a human instinct could be as specialized as that! It is certain that many feelings which appear instinctive are really due to our cultural environment. If any elderly lady could be projected, with her radio or television apparatus, back into the seventeenth century she would be in grave danger of being burned for witchcraft. Her neighbours would feel "instinctively" that there was something unhealthy about it! Enlightened minds in the twentieth century will decline to see the hand of the Devil in the unfamiliar.

In general it may be said that there are customs and attitudes towards death which have been widespread in the past but from which educated people nowadays feel that they ought to free themselves. The black clothing, the pious clichés and euphemisms, the cult of the cemetery—these are matters in which intelligent Christians can afford to be far more rational than is the bulk of mankind. It is not that we have ceased to feel deeply the loss of those we have loved; it is rather that we feel that many outward expressions are hypocritical if there is not genuine grief and pointless if there is.

The simple truth, surely, is this. If we accept the view that physical death necessarily exterminates human personality, we shall regard the attempt to get messages from the departed as not wicked but futile. If, on the other hand, we believe that the departed can survive physical death, then there is nothing more uncanny to a rational mind in the idea that they might be able to communicate with us than in the idea that our friends in America can send us telegrams or talk to us by wireless tele-

K*

phony. I cannot help suspecting that in some cases the prejudice in the matter may be due to a sub-conscious belief, contrary to the creed professed, that the "dead" are really exterminated and that therefore any alleged communications from them *must* be the work of some kind of evil entities. Such a prejudice would be due not to faith but to unbelief.

Another factor tending to prejudice the educated modern mind against spiritualism is its tendency to attract the cranks and the credulous. I recently read, in a journal devoted to psychical matters, an account of a lecture in which it was claimed that nuclear explosions had torn gaps in an etheric envelope which surrounds the earth and that "evil influences" were thus enabled to enter! In view, too, of my criticisms of the notion of reincarnation in Chapter 5, I am entitled to claim as evidence of metaphysical incompetence the light-hearted way in which some, but not all, spiritualists toy with reincarnation in blissful ignorance of its glaring contradiction of views of the life on the "other side" which, when not thinking of reincarnation, they profess to believe on the authority of communications from the departed.

A further source of distrust of spiritualism is the knowledge that a few mediums have been proved fraudulent. Here, again, we ought to avoid initial bias. Very few of those who light-heartedly dismiss the whole business on these grounds have made a patient and scholarly examination of the evidence. Human nature being what it is, one could safely prophesy that even if there are genuine phenomena there will also be fraudulent ones. The existence of fraud, therefore, proves nothing either way. Fraud on the part of "physical" mediums—those who appear to be levitated or to move physical objects—has been exposed on a number of occasions, but it is significant that some of the investigators who found Eusapia Palladino cheating were quite sure that she did not cheat all the time; it is quite natural, after all, to help out one's failing powers with a little deception! I have no emotional urge to believe that physical phenomena of this kind can be genuine, for they seem irrelevant to the question of survival after death, but I am very far from convinced that they are all fraudulent. I find it quite impossible to believe, for example, that had D. D. Home (Browning's "Mr. Sludge") been fraudulent throughout all his amazing career, he would never have been exposed.

The mental phenomena of mediumship, however, are far more important, and only ignorance and prejudice can dismiss them with vague talk or fraud, coincidence or credulity.

But there is one objection to spiritualism with which I feel sympathy. Indeed, I will state it by quoting from a work of my own:[1]

"The reason for expecting that the spiritualist's kind of evidence will not be found compelling is that the only really *worthy* belief in the hereafter, surely, is one which is a corollary of one's whole moral and spiritual philosophy or faith. A wish to prolong the kind of life we live on earth is not particularly creditable or likely to be fulfilled. If one has no faith in God it is foolish to want to survive death. There is, to such a person, no guarantee that the next life will be better than this. And if one does not believe in God—does not believe in any moral government of, or significance in, the Universe—there is no reason to suppose that the survival of death, even by good people, is part of the scheme of things. But the more firmly one believes in God and the more clearly one sees the implications of such a faith, the less need there is for the kind of evidence that spiritualism offers."

Now this is, I still think, a sound *a priori* argument. It certainly indicates that what is at stake in the investigation of spiritualism is not whether the dead can survive but merely whether they can communicate with us. It suggests, indeed, that it may well prove to be the case that they *cannot* communicate with us; it may well be that in the providence of God our faith in survival must have purely moral and spiritual

[1] *The Armour of Saul*, p. 68, James Clarke, London, 1957.

grounds and not be based on any kind of "evidence". But it does not put the question beyond doubt. It has been said that no Englishman is ever fully convinced by an *a priori* argument. The scheme of things is very complex, and as we get older and wiser we tend to distrust sweeping generalizations as to what God would or would not do. We can be sure, of course, that His way is the best, but we are not so confident as we were in our youth that we can always see what *is* best. It may quite well be that in His wisdom He will refuse us evidence for survival, and expect us to believe in it because of our experience of His love. But I cannot see that we can be certain of this until we have investigated the matter.

There is one attitude of mind on this point which I do not think defensible. I can understand a man's preferring to base his belief in the world-to-come on his faith in the love of God and on nothing else. But a person who wants empirical evidence, and who attaches such importance to the resurrection appearances of Jesus as to say that *they* are the basis of his faith, and yet objects to our attempting to get empirical evidence in the twentieth century, is surely inconsistent. Either God is willing to provide empirical evidence or He is not. It is not, of course, impossible, but it seems unlikely that He was willing to give evidence to a tiny group of people long centuries ago and yet refuse it for ever after. My own belief in the world-to-come is based mainly on the moral argument, but I do in fact believe that the resurrection appearances of Jesus were objective. I think it extremely likely, therefore, that visions of the departed experienced in later generations—in our own day, indeed—have been objective too, and I cannot reject out of hand the claim that automatic writings and trance-utterances have contained genuine messages from the departed.

No one who studies human history to get light on the nature of man and on God's dealings with man can fail to see the vast importance of the rise, after the Renaiscence, of the empirical sciences. We must surely see it as the discovery, under the guidance of the Spirit of God, of the correct use of the human reason. It was humbling to realize our limitations—to lose that confidence in the Pure Reason which we had inherited from Plato—or from our misunderstanding of him—and to admit that we must sit down before the despised particular facts; but in its way this brought a *renewal* of confidence in reason, in its inductive or *a posteriori* workings. For the new methods proved amazingly successful.

But can we believe that the new Revelation had no relevance to religion? At the early stage of recorded human history, Divine revelation had been mediated through prophet and law-giver, and accepted as authoritative by the bulk of ordinary men. But can we not believe that God's method of revelation to modern man may be the inspiration and guidance of empirical research in all fields of human speculation? If so, we are bound at least to keep an open mind on the subject of psychical research.

One thing can be said with confidence. If belief in human survival of death is to become universal in the modern world —if, that is, a time is to come when the bulk of men will pre-pare for the hereafter with the same sense of reality as they prepare for their summer holidays—then belief in the hereafter must be established by those methods which have proved so fruitful in all the sciences, including some branches of psycho-logy. If it proves impossible to obtain experimental evidence, then belief in survival will be a minority belief. It will certainly not die out, but it will be the belief of only those whose faith in God is based on first-hand experience and who see clearly that faith in the future life is an integral part of faith in God. There is, of course, New Testament support for the view that people with a vital Christian faith will always be a small minority. "Strait is the gate and narrow the way that leadeth unto life, and few there be that find it". (Matt. vii, 14.) The fact that a belief is held by only a minority has nothing to do with its truth. It ought not to be necessary to utter such a platitude as this, but enthusiasts for Gallup polls sometimes seem to have overlooked it.

It may well prove, then, that in the providence of God man's belief in the hereafter is to be derived solely from his religious and moral convictions. There is nothing unreasonable, let alone absurd, in this. But, on the other hand, it seems possible that that great expansion of knowledge which man has experienced since the discovery of the inductive and constructive use of reason may ultimately include sound empirical evidence for the survival of human personality after death.

Empirical investigation of the type I envisage is, at present, only in its infancy. I must disagree both with the claim that survival has been amply demonstrated and with the statement that no evidence worthy of consideration has ever been obtained. My reasons for dissenting from this last are as follows: Let me begin by pointing out that even if the departed are able to communicate with us when conditions are favourable, we cannot assume that conditions will often be favourable; nor can we assume that the departed are always at our disposal whenever we choose to get in touch. Even on earth we sometimes hesitate to telephone to even our best friends; the telephone can be tyrannical; and, of course, our friends may be out. Again, some of the departed may be more willing, or more able, to communicate than others. If, on casually meeting a clairvoyant, I ask her to put me through to someone on "the other side" I cannot reasonably expect immediate success. Broadly speaking, then, we should expect that the best evidence for survival would be provided soon after the decease of people who, on earth, had been keenly searching for such evidence. One would, indeed, expect that they would take the initiative —that automatic writings and mediumistic utterances would spontaneously offer evidence calculated to convince the friends of the deceased.

Now it seems to me of the utmost importance—so important, indeed, that only prejudice or indifference has prevented the point from being emphasized—to notice that some of the best evidence for survival of death has been obtained just when and where we could, on these general grounds, have expected it. Some of the most striking "communications" have been those purporting to come from some of the deceased founders of the Society for Psychical Research. A complex system of "cross-correspondences" appears to have been devised—not by anyone on earth but from the beyond—with the stated intention of providing an answer to those who have tried to explain away the para-normal knowledge displayed by mediums as due to telepathy from the "sitter". The evidence has been summarized in a number of recent works, including G. N. M. Tyrrell's book to which I have referred, but its cogency cannot be realized by casual reading. The evidence is of a kind which demands scholarly application—the patient and minute sifting of evidence—under the guidance of classical specialists, for some of the alleged communicators, Myers and Verrall, were themselves classical scholars, and it needed a scholar like Piddington to follow the clues.

It has sometimes been suggested that those who have studied the cross-correspondences are in a class with people who produce fantastic clues—anagrams and such-like—proving that Bacon wrote Shakespeare's plays. There really is no analogy between the two classes. The extreme improbability of Bacon's having behaved in this fantastic manner is obvious; the procedure seems pointless. But it is quite on the cards that a keen mind such as Myers's, if anxious to communicate evidence and realizing the use that was being made of the telepathy interpretation, should have tried to circumvent that interpretation. The method employed was ingenious in the extreme, and only obvious after the event, like Columbus's method of standing an egg on end.

One criticism of mediumistic communications is that they often exhibit the inconsequence of dreams; the evidential images and symbols occur as items in a chain of irrelevancies, and the links of the chain are largely arbitrary, even verbal, associations of ideas rather than logical connections. But this criticism carries weight only if we make some quite *a priori* assumptions. It is not for us to decide in advance what the machinery of communication must be. The analogy of the long-distant telephone is quite misleading. The process must, in any case, be complicated, and if the alleged communications are genuine they seem to depend on the communicator's exercising some sort of influence on the flow of such dream-imagery as the particular medium happens to be capable of; this, of course, limits him greatly.

My own view is that there is a strong *prima facie* case for the thesis that genuine communications have been made. Mrs. Sidgwick, who brought a keenly critical mind to the study of the subject and who pursued it with admirable patience and thoroughness, was finally convinced that evidence had been provided that human individuals can survive death and can communicate with us. I must confess myself greatly impressed by the cross-correspondences, including the *Palm Sunday case* recently reported in the Proceedings of the Society for Psychical Research, and also by the work of the late Rev. C. Drayton Thomas, whom I knew when I was a curate in Bromley, Kent, and who let me listen to recordings of some of his sittings with Mrs. Leonard.

I must here offer a protest against the casual and careless dismissal of the para-normal element in the utterances of mediums as "due to telepathy from the living". The word "telepathy" has no more claim to be an explanation than has the word "instinct". Both are merely labels for our ignorance. Very little, if any, light is thrown on the powers of mediums by the discovery that certain people have para-normal card-guessing powers. In these card-guessing experiments, one person is co-operating in an attempt to see whether he can influence the mind of another person. Few people seem to have any appreciable powers of giving or receiving information in this way, but in any case the "telepathy" evidenced by these experiments is on a very different scale from that evidenced by mediums. If the phenomena of the so-called mediumistic trance, including cases where the medium communicates facts never known by the "sitter", are to be explained as telepathy from those living on earth, one must postulate a type of telepathy far more remarkable than that evidenced by the card-guessing experiments. The medium must be able to select, from the vast population around her, the person who possesses the required knowledge! Now, the reply usually made to this objection is that if we admit para-normal powers at all, it is not for us to set limits to them. This would be a fair reply to the suggestion that such a power of selection was *impossible*. But it misses the mark here, for the argument is that no scientist, working on his own subject, prefers a complex to a simple explanation, and prefers to postulate *ad hoc* existence of something not otherwise evidenced when he can appeal to something familiar. In the Chaffin Will case, for example, it is far *simpler* to suppose that the deceased Mr. Chaffin was revealing the fact that he had made a later will than that his son possessed some mysterious power of finding what it was to his advantage to find. And the simpler explanation has the additional advantage of appealing to a power independently known to exist—that of *imparting* information. One could reasonably prefer the complex explanation, the postulation *ad hoc* of something otherwise unevidenced, only if one had been convinced *on other grounds* that survival was impossible. The Chaffin Will case, approached without initial bias, certainly favours the survival hypothesis.

There have been cases in which a deceased person has left a sealed envelope containing information not known by normal means to any living person. I know of two cases which were conclusive neither way—they were neither complete failures nor successes. It is important to realize that in such cases the element of failure presents a problem for the believer in *any* theory which accounts for the para-normal knowledge displayed by sensitives. If successful mediumship is to be explained as the display of extraordinary powers of *selective* clairvoyance or telepathy, these two cases show that sometimes the powers fail. Similarly, if we explain it as the power or receiving messages from the departed. Clearly, we must suspend judgment.

The whole study, in short, is in its infancy, and has hitherto been made on a very small scale. The vast majority of people are either indifferent or hostile—indifferent because passively materialistic, or hostile either because actively materialistic or on religious grounds. It is all the more remarkable, then, that such outstanding sensitives as Mrs. Piper and Mrs. Leonard and many others—including the ladies who communicated the cross-correspondences—have been discovered.

The churches certainly ought to take a much more active interest in this matter. There is evidence that in the early Church great importance was attached to the utterances of psychics. We are right to appeal to St. Paul's insistence that charity is of greater importance than "prophesying", and we should have to be on our guard lest concern with the hereafter should become an obsession, diverting us from a healthy concern with earthly life and duties. But the whole burden of this book is that only in the light of a living faith in a world-to-come can we make moral sense of earthly life and live as we ought to. If that is true—and I cannot see how any Christian can deny it—then psychical research could help to make us better citizens of *this* world.

I should not care to prophesy whether communications from the departed will ever provide us with a detailed picture of life "on the other side", or challenge or augment our Christian eschatology. The edifying addresses given by entranced mediums are unevidential; they may well have their sole source in the medium's mind. It would seem that in the nature of things evidence that some particular person has survived physical death must relate to details, prosaic and trivial in themselves and of no spiritual value, but of the kind which only he can have known, and which can be verified.

Is belief that the departed can communicate the fact of their existence to us incompatible with belief in the traditional heaven and hell, with purgatory, with universalism or with conditional immortality? My answer is that if we are going to employ the empirical method we must be patient. I feel that

I have enough to live by if I can believe that God has some great moral purpose in placing us in this world and that in this life we are given the opportunity of receiving the free gift of life eternal. And I have one conviction so deep-seated that I should reject any alleged message from the beyond which denied it. This is that in some sense our entry into the life of the world to come must entail *judgment*; we shall reap what we sow. Wages of sin in *some* sense there must be. I should, of course, like to believe in universalism, the doctrine that *ultimately* everyone will be saved, but I cannot honestly say I *do* believe it. There is, indeed, in my view one consideration which favours the belief in conditional immortality. Let us consider.

Before the discovery of the evolution of the human species from lower forms of life it was easy to say that human beings, as such, are inherently immortal, whereas animals are not. But if we hold that animals are mortal, and also hold that it is impossible to select a definite date at which the human species started, are we not in for a difficulty if we say that humans are immortal and animals mortal? One way out would be to say that animals, too, survive the death of their bodies, but this involves us in difficulties which appear to me insuperable. Firstly, an entity cannot *continue* to exist if it has not even begun to exist. A study of comparative psychology makes it extremely doubtful whether even the highest of the animals are to any appreciable extent capable of explicit memory—of free images. They possess *some* degree of intelligence, admittedly; they have some capacity for learning from experience, and this means that their past experiences must have left some trace which can in some way colour their present experiences and so cause a variation in response. But it is very doubtful whether they are more than subconsciously and dimly aware of anything more than the *feeling-tone* of the past experience —whether pleasure which encourages repetition of the action producing the experience or pain which inhibits it. There is no reason to suppose that the dog says to himself, "Last time I did so-and-so I got a beating for it".

Now if there is no explicit memory and therefore so self-consciousness, personality has not been created. As we saw in Chapter 5, memory and self-consciousness are essential to personal identity and permanence. An animal is not in this sense a person; it lives in the present; it does not "look before and after"; it is little more than a machine which makes the same reaction whenever the same button is pushed.

There can be no question, then, of the survival of animal personality, for an animal is not a person. Besides, where is the line going to be drawn? Can you seriously entertain the notion of the immortality of a jelly-fish, or a cholera germ?

The second difficulty in the notion of animal survival is this. It seems as clear as anything can be that a being incapable of self-consciousness and explicit memory has not *moral* consciousness. When the dog slinks away after raiding the larder it is not accurate to say, "He knows he has done wrong". His reaction can be quite adequately explained as due to fear. The moral argument for survival, then, does not apply to animal life.

We are back, then, to our original point. At one point in evolutionary history did immortality begin? It would seem that the line between mortal and immortal beings is not one drawn between all members of the species born before a certain date and all born after it. The answer could well be that human beings are, and remain, animals until *in some sense* they are "born again". A quite clear-cut line could be drawn—by God, of course, not by us! My present argument is very far from being the presumptuous attempt to say how God does, still less how He ought to, draw the line; it is merely concerned to show that even though man is continuous with the animals, in such wise that it is difficult to say that all men, as such, are immortal, nevertheless there is no difficulty in seeing how a line *could* be drawn. It could be drawn not between animals and men but between men, between those who have in some sense been "born again" and those who have not. The class of those born again would include those who have received the new birth in

Christ in the New Testament sense, but it would surely not be restricted to these. Any men who can be said to be seeking God, whether they explicitly realize it or not, any who can conceive of the possibility of a higher, a more moral and more spiritual life than we attain in this life and who deeply desire it—these, we may surely believe, will receive the gift of eternal life.

The charge of pride or presumption has been brought against those who hope for their own eternal salvation and yet who cannot affirm their belief in universalism—the belief that ultimately all men will be saved. But the Christian has a complete answer. His confidence in his acceptance with God is based not on his merits—not on any conviction that he has *earned* salvation—but on God's grace. Even if he will have no truck with Calvinism he can point out that there is no merit in accepting a free gift of forgiveness. If he is a Calvinist—as I think deeper thinkers must be, to the extent of seeing that man's freedom and God's sovereign election are not, for a sound personalist metaphysics such as I have outlined, antithetical—then he can with even greater confidence rebut the charge of pride. It was precisely because Calvin did not claim to be better than anyone else by nature that he appealed to God's sovereign election.[2]

My difficulty with universalism—the doctrine that ultimately everyone will be "saved"—is rooted in my recognition that Christian theology must be empirical and dualistic, as I have argued in Chapter 6. I cannot feel happy with the argument that unless everyone is ultimately saved we shall have the contradictory situation that God's purposes are defeated. Not only is it an *a priori* argument of the kind I distrust, but it does not seem to do justice to the empirical reality of evil and the fact of man's moral responsibility. If a morally responsible being announces that he does not want a higher and better life—that he is content with what this world offers—then I cannot see that his extermination at physical death offers any greater

[2] I have discussed the problem of man's freedom and God's sovereignty in *God, Man and the Absolute*, Chapter 4. (Hutchinson, 1947) and in *Christian Rationalism and Philosophical Analysis*, Chapter 10 (James Clarke, 1959).

moral problem than does the fact that animals who, equally, do not desire a higher life, are exterminated.

On general grounds, then, there seems much to be said for the doctrine of conditional immortality. But beyond that I cannot go; it is not for us to dogmatize. But this conclusion does tempt me to offer one final generalization in this matter of the relation between psychical research and Christian eschatology. It is this: Evidence of the kind which confines itself to establishing the continued existence of the departed—the furnishing of matter-of-fact details which only the departed could have known and which can be verified—will be accepted by all honest people provided it is cogent enough. But messages purporting to convey information as to the nature of life beyond the grave will have, if they are to convince us, to rise far above the cheap and cheerful eschatology offered by certain types (I do not say all types) of spiritualism. As I said, there is evidence that the early Church held in honour people with psychic gifts. But the first epistle of St. John warns us to "believe not every spirit, but try the spirits whether they are of God".

Conclusion

IT SEEMS to me that the foregoing argument has two practical implications, one with regard to the teaching of religion to children and the other with regard to the visible unity of the Church.

In my view, the religious instruction of children needs drastic overhauling. Here I can only state two broad principles. First, that while recognizing that the instruction of each age-group must be adapted to its learning-capacity, we must, nevertheless, aim at preventing a situation arising in which adolescents become aware that what they were told at an earlier stage was not strictly true. Small children have to be told stories, but in my experience even young children can take the point that the story is "only a story", and their enjoyment and edification is in no sense diminished thereby.

The second principle is that the order of instruction of the individual should follow the Divine order of the Hebrew and Christian revelation; the law must precede the gospel. The main aim with children should be instruction in the principles of conduct—the conditioning of their reflexes, if you prefer the modern phrase. It will be clear from my third chapter that this instruction should have a theistic basis; the moral law must be taught as God's law. But the Christian child must not start with the notion of a sentimental God and a "nice" world, and then awake later to grimmer realities with a shock. It is far better that there should be an element of austerity from the start. Surprises there are bound to be when, in his late teens, he

comes to take a more synoptic view of life, but it will be far
better if he discovers the gospel of love as a reaction from
austerity than if he discovers reality in reaction from senti-
mentality.

With the regard to the unity of Christendom, it is surely
clear that the main work has to be done in the study by scholars, not in the conference room by ecclesiastics. If I believe
that our Lord himself taught episcopacy or presbyterianism or
independency, then I *cannot* compromise. I am right and the
others wrong. Re-union cannot come, and ought not to come,
unless we are convinced that the things which divide us are
unimportant and are not matters of Divine injunction. If what
I have written helps anyone to reach such a conviction it will
not have been written in vain.

Index

The author of this book is a member of the Council of the Modern Churchmen's Union, and he has written it from a convicition that the case for liberal Christianity and Christian humanism needs re-stating in the light of the changes in the climate of thought since the Union was formed in 1898.

In philosophy there has been a tendency to replace metaphysics by language analysis, with a consequent dismissal of all philosophical theology based on reason. Certain theologians have welcomed this as in line with their own attack on the human reason, involved in their attack on Christian humanism, and they have sought to return to Reformation theology with its insistence on "The Fall" and on human depravity, basing the Faith not on experience and reason but on a view of the authority of Scripture which it is hard to reconcile with the results of historical criticism. The author has tried to state the case for liberal Christianity with these trends of thought in mind.

With the increased interest in comparative religion has come an attack from certain quarters on the Christian doctrine of the value of the empirical individual—a doctrine which the author holds to be among the most important contributions to world religion made by Christianity. He devotes a chapter to this. He closes with a discussion of the bearing of psychical research on the Christian view of the life of the world to come—a subject which can no longer be ignored now that this research has been recognised in British and American universities as a valid department of scientific psychology.